The Future Path of SMEs

The Future Path of SMEs

How to Grow in the New Global Economy

Prof. Amr Sukkar, PhD, MPhil, MBA

BEP

BUSINESS EXPERT PRESS

Leader in applied, concise business books

The Future Path of SMEs: How to Grow in the New Global Economy

Copyright © Business Expert Press, LLC, 2023.

Cover design by Charlene Kronstedt

Interior design by Exeter Premedia Services Private Ltd., Chennai, India

First published in 2022 by
Business Expert Press, LLC
222 East 46th Street, New York, NY 10017
www.businessexpertpress.com

ISBN-13: 978-1-63742-281-6 (paperback)
ISBN-13: 978-1-63742-282-3 (e-book)

Business Expert Press Economics and Public Policy Collection

First edition: 2022

10 9 8 7 6 5 4 3 2 1

Description

Most of businesses fall within the category of start-up, small and medium size enterprises. Therefore, governments in part of their quest to reform the economy and related regulatory management systems as well as the entrepreneurship support ecosystem. This was done with a view to securing the national governance empowerment deemed necessary for the economic and political fostering, adaptation, growth and progress of this sector.

These endeavors serve as an essential part of the economic reform needed to generally guide the economy to a balanced and sustained growth vision. This vision aims specifically at achieving a balanced and diversified skill-based economy that is ultimately dependent on knowledge, innovation and competitiveness. This obviously arises from the ventures of entrepreneurs, startups as well as small and medium size enterprises (SMEs).

In this context, this book tries to support the elaboration and implementation of strategies and to foster SMEs and entrepreneurship development. This will include contribution to set a guide to illustrate the scientific way for the identification of stakeholders and dialogue platforms as well as the institutionalization of the processes and systems required to improve the regulatory framework for SME development.

The book also provides the consultancy effort needed to support governments in setting targets for SME policy development and to identify strategic priorities to further improve the business environment.

Keywords

global economy; SME; entrepreneurship; competitiveness; policy development; stakeholders; strategy; startups; nationalization; entrepreneurial mindset; small and medium enterprises; SME mindset; innovation

Contents

Preface

Economic policy is a broad-ranging discipline, with regard to both the question it asks and the methods it uses to seek an answer. Rather than trying to define the discipline in a single sentence or paragraph, we will introduce you to economic policy in the SME context by letting the subject matter speak for itself. Many-worlds most pressing problems are economic in nature.

In this book, we try to give you some ideas of the sorts of issues that SMEs economic policy analysis helps to clarify and the kinds of solutions and development that SMEs economic principles suggest. We try also to introduce the tools that economists and policy makers use. You are likely to find them useful in your career and your personal life. Economic policies, as we believe, are a way of thinking, not a fixed body of facts or knowledge to be memorized. The objective of this book is to help readers, researchers, professionals, or students understand, not memorize, these principles and guide them on how to apply them to a variety of SMEs' economic problems and issues.

Preface

Acknowledgments

I would like to express my gratitude and appreciation for the people who helped and supported me until I finished this work. I also wish to extend heartfelt thanks to my family, especially my wife, for their ongoing support and understanding.

CHAPTER 1

Introduction and Overview

Small and medium-sized enterprises, commonly known as SMEs, have for quite some time been acknowledged as the motors of monetary development and advancement. Why? This is due to the effect of SMEs on worldwide economy and the significant role they play in the structure of the general public, which is liberated from neediness. They provide sufficient openings for work to the different sectors of the general public. Technology as well as SMEs assume a significant role in worldwide economy. We put great emphasis on the foreign direct investment (FDI) of small technology-based firms and how their innovations diffuse into the global economy.

The question is how economic action is affecting the direction of globalization. With the evolvement of the 21st century, a worldwide system of production and distribution is developing in the same way national markets changed from local and regional networks during the 19th century (Chandler 1990). Stocks have augmented relative to total investment and gross national product in nearly every country (Dunning 1995). Globalization refers to the network of relations and interconnections between states, societies, and organizations that structure the present world economic system. The development of global business sectors animates rivalry and powers governments to embrace market-arranged policies, both locally and internationally. Modern technologies have greatly reduced the cost of information and the capabilities to participate in the global economy (Dunning 1993). Alongside with the globalization trend, contemporary technical advances are demanding synthesis and more integration between innovative and productive activities. The pressures of global competition force producers to continually innovate and upgrade the quality of existing products. However, many firms can no longer acquire or afford all the technological and human resources that they need. Increasingly, they form interdependent and flexible relationships with other firms—including suppliers and competing firms—to fully capitalize on their core competencies (Gomes-Casseres 1996). Interdependence calls for a capacity on the part of firms, individuals, and governments to interact with speed, flexibility, and creativity with the actions of other agents (De la Mothe and Paquet 1996) Firms must develop human resource strategies based on synthesis with educational institutions. The critical feature of strategic asset-seeking FDI, as opposed to market-seeking FDI, is that participating firms recognize that their standalone resources and abilities are inadequate to sustain their international competitiveness and that they need to draw upon resources and capabilities of others to reach this goal. There are many reasons why firms form alliances with other firms.

According to conventional wisdom, most transnational business activities, particularly those involving FDI or cross-border alliances, are traditionally carried out by large firms. Hence, some people have believed that technological transformation requires increasingly large-scale operations, along with increasing the size of research and development (R&D) resources. These views would lead one to expect that small enterprises would decline in importance as they become overwhelmed by global firms exploiting economies of scale. There is considerable evidence that these commonly held views are no longer correct. With the issue of business size measure revisited, the long-term trend toward increasing firm size either decelerated, ceased, or overturned itself sometime between the late 1960s and the late 1970s (Acs 1996). This leads to the interesting question of whether the apparent resurgence of smaller firms is due to the emergence of a dynamic, vital, and innovative entrepreneurial sector, or it is due to the inability of large obligatory multinational enterprises (MNEs) to prevail in a technologically active global environment.

Harrison (1994) argues that the role of SMEs has been overestimated, and that MNEs have been able to prosper in the new global environment by combining four simple building blocks: returning to their core competencies, using new information technologies, forming strategic alliances, and eliciting more active collaboration from their workers. This view, though, overlooks the synergy between large and small firms, the strong attachment of small firms to their local economies, the role of small firms in technological change, and the role they play in the growth and evolution of industries (Acs 1996).

Hence, the Center for International Business Education and Research (CIBER) at the University of Maryland organized a discussion of experts on "Small and Medium Sized Enterprises and the Global Economy," which was held on October 20, 1995. The primary focus of the conference was on the role that technology and network organizations play in the global activities of SMEs. Members in this conference studied the role of SMEs in the identification of technological opportunity, technological diversity, geographical localization, technology transfer, R&D spillovers, strategic alliances and the international diffusion of innovations. An overview of SMEs participation in the global economy reveals at least three lines of activity: trade, technology, and investment. The most commonly discussed topic in SMEs is export activity as linked to the other activities that are given greater emphasis here. The second most prominent issue in the literature is SMEs and technology, and mainly SME supplier connections with larger MNEs in local markets. In their simplest form, these connections involve intra-national exports, that is, domestic sales to foreign firms, which happen to be operating within the home country of the supplier. The emphasis was mostly on the transfer of technology from MNEs to their SME suppliers and consumers, although it was also acknowledged that MNEs might acquire the appropriate technology from local SMEs and possibly eventually acquire the SME firms themselves as well. The final issue is the role of SMEs in investment—the connection between SMEs and FDI. SMEs may evolve as multinationals either through their own investments or as a result of the formation of alliances. We start by examining the technological basis of SMEs. Though in the aggregate, SMEs spend less on R&D than large firms, they produce almost twice as many innovations on the per employee basis (Acs and Audretsch 1990). In 1993 in the United States, SMEs received 3.8 percent of federal R&D dollars and performed 14.5 percent of company funded industrial R&D (U.S. National Science Foundation 1996). In 1991, SMEs received 40 percent of all domestic utility patents granted in the U.S. Patent and Trademark Office. Recently, Cohen and Klepper (1996) have suggested that while small firms may be superior in the generation of new knowledge, larger firms are superior in their ability to appropriate returns from these innovations, either by buying property rights, acquiring the firms, or benefiting through spillovers. This raised two important questions:

1. Why are SMEs superior innovators in the first place?
2. How do we explain the higher innovative performance of SMEs if they spend less on R&D than large firms?

The critical role of property rights in capitalist economies is becoming more and more evident. Societies must protect trendsetters' property rights to the gains from their innovations. An additional angle is that it also emphasizes an innovator's property rights within an organization. An innovator in a large company only has very limited property right protection. The new product, process, and so on generally belong to the firm, not the employee who invented it. This reduces creative employees' incentives to innovate for the company. The lack of clear property rights in large corporations creates perverse incentives for both employees and managers. Both can benefit from *free riding* on other people's innovative efforts and results.

In contrast to innovative employees in large firms, independent innovators can hold clear property rights, can have every incentive to undertake radical innovations, and can be largely free of red tape. Thus, they argue that SMEs are better at making radical innovations because they better protect the innovator's property rights. Ketkar and Acs (2013) further argue that the international diffusion of SME innovations is very important for global economic welfare. However, SMEs have only limited operations abroad. One reason for this is barriers to entry. Barriers to entry that limit international expansion are systematically higher for SMEs than for larger firms. The other reason is that SMEs have less resources to protect their property rights. The authors suggest that these problems faced by SMEs in international markets can frequently be circumvented by using existing MNEs as international conduits for SME innovations. Lately, SMEs have enlisted a higher development rate when contrasted with the worldwide mechanical area. The main preferred position of the SME area is its capability to create work at low capital consumption.

MNEs can, thus, be catalysts and facilitators of smaller firms international expansion. While direct expansion by SMEs is the subject of much discussion, the intermediated possibility has not been given much attention. However, such intermediated modes of expansion are adversely affected by transaction difficulties and intermediator's rent extraction, which are topics explored in greater details in Gomes-Casseres, Kohn, and Eden's papers. Ketkar and Acs (2013) raise several conceptual considerations important in comparing the two modes of international expansion and identifying the conditions for private market arrangements to be efficient. They do not believe direct subsidies to SMEs going abroad are advisable.

How do we explain the superior innovative performance of SMEs? In a recent study, Jaffe, Trajtenberg, and Henderson (1993) analyze patent citation data pertaining to domestic university and corporate patents to test the extent of the localization of knowledge spillovers. Almeida and Kogut (1997) found that localization of patentable knowledge varies across regions. Semiconductor knowledge in the Silicon Valley and New York triangle tends to be localized. This suggests that complementarities are important (Feldman and Audretsch 1996). Recent literature has suggested that SMEs benefit from R&D spillovers from university research and private research at large firms, but why would this phenomenon of regional organizing advantage more modest firms as opposed to bigger ones? One reason, perhaps, is that larger firms, because of their property rights and incentive structure, are more self-reliant and do not emphasize building relationships with other institutions in the region. By definition, in a start-up, the personnel in a new company will have a shorter tenure in the company and recent experience in other firms. To study the influence of geographic localization and technological diversity on innovation, Almeida and Kogut (1997) examine the origins of citations to 170 major patents in the semiconductor industry. Field research, consisting of interviews with semiconductor engineers and other informed individuals, served to complement the patent analysis. They argue that:

1. Start-ups gain their comparative innovative advantage by exploring new technological spaces that may be overlooked by larger firms.

2. This process is facilitated by regional networking, which permits small firms to obtain and use knowledge more efficiently than large firms.

They find that new businesses produce developments in less jam-packed innovative space than bigger firms. That is, little firms are bound to investigate automatically in different regions. While information is contained for both new businesses and different firms, new companies are all the more intently integrated with local organizations because they rely upon networks for genuine information inputs. Information was more restricted for new businesses than different firms with gatherings of business people assuming an urgent job. This is the neighborhood character of the organizations—that is, their conceivable connection with globalization. Small technology-based firms are more attractive acquisition targets for MNEs interested in entering new technological networks.

Almost 10 percent of the 38,000 new high-tech establishments listed in the Corp Tech database had foreign ownership in 1994 (Science and Engineering Indicators 1996, 6–29). If small firms face difficult barriers to entry in international operations than large firms and have a more difficult time protecting their property rights, how can they become international companies? When SMEs invest abroad, they generally look for help. Gomes-Casseres (1996) surveys the use of strategic alliances by SMEs. He asks three questions:

1. When do small firms use alliances to do business in a foreign country?
2. How do small businesses use agreements?
3. What effect do alliances have on firm competitive performance?

The researchers define a new unit of competition called a constellation. A constellation is a set of firms linked together by alliances. The researchers find that small firms can follow one of two different approaches to alliances, depending on their comparative size. Firms that are small relative to competitors and to the requirements of the market tend to use alliances to reach scale and scope economies. Firms that are large, relative to the same benchmark, trust on internal capabilities to expand. In any event, the evidence shows that SMEs, against the expectations of many traditional scholars, are active players in the international arena. Kohn and Hüsig (2006) studied how SMEs deal with the international game when they choose not to collaborate with larger partners. They discovered that most small multinational firms follow a deep position strategy. Their positions were characterized by market power and technological leadership and by a focus on producer goods. In addition, small firms prefer to invest in earlier industries than more mature ones. In fact, Gomes-Casseres and Kohn (forthcoming) find that SMEs have had smaller amount of alliances than one might have expected.

Do SMEs face higher transaction costs than MNEs in international expansion? Eden, Levitas, and Martinez (1997) survey a large literature dealing with international business, entrepreneurship, and technical change, and they provide a link between the technological literature on SMEs and the technological literature on MNEs. This examines three aspects of technology:

1. Technology as a firm-specific benefit
2. The costs of technology transfer
3. Technology spillovers

They prescribe that SMEs are less inclined to have the option to appropriately manage the innovation move measure when issues occur. About the expenses of the innovation move, they suggest that SMEs may face higher transaction costs than large MNEs because they also have fewer resources to dedicate to search, negotiation, monitoring, and enforcement efforts. They may also be more subject to opportunistic behavior on the part of suppliers and buyers due to their smaller size and corresponding inability to retaliate. The worldwide dispersion of new advancements is vital for proceeding with the progress of worldwide monetary government assistance. The analysis suggests that policies should aim to reduce the costs in international expansion for SMEs. That is, policies should aim to reduce the private market costs incurred to protect property rights and to reduce entry barriers, and transaction costs should be less in amount.

To rival worldwide competition and conquer the fast innovation change and item assortment development in the new assembling climate,

SMEs must have the option to proceed in item advancement (Laforet 2008). It is just with exactness and care that the legislature can energize business by making business-accommodating strategies and simple financing alternatives. Liberal strategies urge imminent business people to dive in and make an incentive for themselves just as a society eventually.

CHAPTER 2

New Global Economy and SMEs

Introduction

Nowadays, global economy encourages limited-sized enterprises through providing new opportunities for further expansion and development. Proving to have an impact on all economic activities is necessary for business survival in the global market. Hence, SMEs are directing their business onto the internationalization concept to achieve competitiveness in the global market in addition to overcome their limitations. Turning the business scope from a closed market to a global market is crucial to compete in the business field taking into account the obstacles that SMEs face as an exporter or direct investor and how to overcome those obstacles. As a consequence, this chapter handles how successful entrepreneurs build internationalization strategies to overcome any constraints as well as deal with foreign market barriers. Moreover, variable economic activities are also identified in this chapter.

Globalization

Globalization refers to the web of interconnections and linkages between organizations, states, and societies that make up the economic system of the present world. Globalization develops new relationships and new structures with the result that business decisions and actions in one part of the world have consequences in other places. Underlying and reinforcing these globalization trends are information processing, telecommunications, and the rapidly changing technological environment, particularly in biotechnology (Acs and Preston 1997).

Globalization is hardly a new phenomenon. After all international trade, management and labor, direct foreign investment, and the associated movement of capital have been going on for centuries. Belchamber of the Australian Council of Trade Unions argues that they found a close linkage between the interests of firms like the East India Company and the interests of nations (Belchamber 1995). However defined, there seems to be general agreement that the pace of such activities has increased. "Total world trade in goods and services has expanded year after year, with few interruptions, for more than four decades" (EPAC 1995a, 13).

There is no specific way to identify a single key factor as the primary motivator for this interest and increase in globalization. Three main factors, however, have been identified (EPAC 1995a, 4). They are:

1. Technological improvements
2. A higher global outlook at firm level
3. Government policy initiatives in developed and developing countries

The global market growth stimulates competition as it forces governments to adopt market-oriented policies, both internationally and domestically. Modern technologies have minimized greatly the cost of information and have enhanced the capabilities to participate in the global economy (Dunning 1993). As globalization is defined by being the broader opening up of national economies to the international marketplace, it has implications for small firms as well as large ones. Increasing the participation of small firms in the international marketplace is an important part of globalization. (Graham 1999).

Acs (1996) argues that in the recent century, all economic activity types are directed into globalization. Since the 19th century, many national markets have been evolved into global markets (Chandler 1990). Dunning (1995) confirms the dramatic increase in both the inbound and outbound FDI stocks in almost every country. As a consequence, FDI is increased at a more rapid rate than international trade. SMEs account for about 80 percent of the global economic growth. Hence, SMEs are considered the cornerstone of the global economy (Jutla, Bodorik, and Dhaliwal 2002). Changing the technological environment due to global competition has a great force to elevate innovation and the quality of the products. This leads many firms that have problems affording technological upgrading systems to make relationships with other corporates to capitalize on their core competencies (Gomes-Casseres 1996). Harrison (1994) discusses the new global environment mentioning the return on the competitive value, which results from using recent technologies, forming critical alliances, and finally, obtaining more active teamwork collaboration. It has been witnessed that larger markets favor larger firms. Thus, partnership alliances are the new trend in most business sectors, especially for those who are seeking internationalization. Hence, this chapter handles the factors promoting globalization in addition to highlighting and promoting resources on strategic projects while endorsing the guiding principles.

SMEs: The Internationalization Process and Performance

SMEs have been recently endorsing the new business trend of internationalization believing that diversification plays a strategic important role (Coviello, McDougall, and Oviatt 1994, 1999). SME internationalization is affected directly by two major forces: government barrier decline and advanced technologies. Customer needs and wants were in a rapid dynamic change during the past decades in response to the aggressive high-tech competitions. Technology and innovation have diversified market demands by introducing the most updated technological and innovative products and services (Rafinejad 2007). High-tech applied sciences are converted into economic profits leading to local economic development (Van Roy and Nepelski 2017). The major key factor leading to the success of high-tech projects in any market is the emergence of local enterprises with international enterprises resulting in "[e]xpansion through [i]nternationalization" that could be done by adopting either of the following strategies: "[i] nternational [s]trategy, [m]ulti domestic [s]trategy, [g]lobal [s]trategy, [t] ransnational [s]trategy." Professor Daniel Isenberg (2011) outlined several *prescriptions* for the ecosystem formation in high-tech entrepreneurship. The first prescription was to stop imitating Silicon Valley, the headquarter of innovation and technology, where Apple, Google, Netflix, and so on are located. The second prescription was to build the ecosystem while considering local conditions and reforming the existing industries rather than starting from scratch. The third prescription was engaging the private sector with the governmental sector while stressing the latter's indirect role as a facilitator only not a directing manager (www.weforum.org). Sodagar (2006) mentions in his book that seeking high-tech industrialization is the turning point of economic development. High-tech projects may drive entrepreneurs to many horizons, leading to further development. For example, as seen nowadays, the Corona (COVID-19) pandemic outbreak has inspired several technological inventions that include a human-sized nursing robot made for dealing with infected patients (www.see-news.net).

Challenges of Technological Change

Human resources associated with technological entrepreneurship must have specialized skills linked to their ability of understanding sciences and implementing technological development that add value to the firm (www.timreview.ca). However, it is a must to invest in developing technical support to ensure the establishment as well as the security of the newly performed high-tech projects. There is a dire need for training a new array of highly talented young leaders with strategic thinking who are capable of managing and operating technological enterprises for the upcoming decades. Moreover, recent sciences have stated that introducing innovation to product development through establishing high-tech ventures cannot be effective without applying the project management approach (Pokharel, Yeo, and Wang 2006).

SMEs Geographic Expansion

Geographic expansion is the most important step toward globalization strategy leading the firm to grow rapidly by broadening customer bases (Barringer and Greening 1998). Despite the value created through geographic expansion, there are many challenges that remain as constraints. Typically those challenges are associated with the liabilities of foreignness and newness (Stinchcombe 1965). However, the previous studies focused on exporting activities *behaviors and strategies*. More recently, economists have extended the investigation to include SMEs foreign investments and firm performance. Hence, it is concluded that the two major avenues in global economy and firm internationalization are both exporting and FDI activities.

Exporting is the paving path to enter different markets for future SMEs international expansion. Obviously, several scale and scope economies are obtained by exporting. In addition, the presence of variant international markets can increase the capacity of potential markets and also can increase business revenues (DeSarbo et al. 1992).

FDI is the direct capital investment activity in foreign countries. Although exporting is less dangerous than FDI, many investors prefer FDI over exporting because it minimizes the property risk in asset exchange through internalizing markets. FDI promotes location-based advantages such as competitive labor price, resource availability, and knowledge diversification. FDI investors are committed to financing a high level of resources, which makes it difficult to reverse the exporting activity. In addition, political instability is considered an important issue for FDI investors.

Alliances: When SMEs do not have the capability to adopt the full range of resources accompanied by FDI, alliances are suggested to overcome the shortage in resources. Previous literature on alliances points to several interests, including the decrease in transaction costs, high market power, reduced risks, and greater availability of resources such as capital and information. The real limitation in expanding the firm through alliances is to find the right partner. "A firm has three basic partner choices: it can cooperate with firms from the host country, with firms from the home country, or with firms from a third country" (Makino and Delios 1996).

Startups and Small- and Medium-Sized Enterprises (SMEs)

SMEs are defined by the Organization for Economic Cooperation and Development (OECD) (2004) as independent, nonsubsidiary firms that have less than a given number of employees. The most frequent upper limit of employees is 250. In other cases, financial criteria such as balance sheet valuations or turnover are used. Within the OECD, it is estimated that SMEs weigh 95 percent of all businesses and 60 to 70 percent of employment. Albeit crude, these figures show the importance of SMEs to modern economy. A more salient feature and characteristic is the flourishing internationalization of these enterprises as an effect of the integration process and technological change (Johnson and Turner 2010).

The importance of SMEs to global economy is shown through their:

- Contribution to employment: the labor-intensive nature of many SMEs and their comparatively rapid growth shows the importance of SMEs to job generation
- Role in the streamlining and restructuring of large state-owned businesses: SMEs help in the sale of noncore production activities and absorption of redundant employees
- Innovatory capacity: there is a school of thought that believes that SMEs need to be more creative to survive, especially in knowledge-intensive sectors such as biotechnology and IT
- Capability to export: this will be a key issue, though most do not tend to engage in international activities
- Greater flexibility in the provision of services and the manufacture of a variety of consumer goods
- Contribution to the competitiveness of the marketplace and their challenge to the monopolistic positions of large enterprises
- Potential role as seedbeds for the development of entrepreneurial skills and innovation
- Their role in the provision of services in the community and in regional development program

Other contributions include the possession of management structures and the augmentation of consumer choices through the production of a greater diversity of specialized goods and services, which makes them more agile (Johnson and Turner 2010).

Globalization and SMEs

The CIBER organized a conference of experts on "SMEs and the Global Economy," which was held on October 20, 1995 (Acs and Preston 1997).

The primary focus of the conference was on the role that technology and network organizations play in the global activities of SMEs. Participants in this conference surveyed the act of SMEs in the identification of technological opportunity, technological diversity, geographical localization, technology transference, R&D spillovers, strategic affiliation, and the international diffusion of innovations (Acs and Preston 1997).

An overview of SME participation in the global economy showed at least three lines of activity: investment, trade, and technology. The topic that had the highest discussion in SMEs international literature was their contribution as exporters from their domestic jurisdictions to foreign customers. The opportunities and challenges facing SMEs in this contribution are well known (Acs and Preston 1997).

The second most dramatic issue is SMEs and technology, and particularly SME supplier connections with larger MNEs in local markets. In their simplest form, these connections involve *intra-national exports*, that is, domestic sales to foreign firms, who happen to be operating within the home country of the supplier. These connections came up for explicit attention at the conference primarily in connection with technological opportunity, technological diversity, technology transfer, and R&D spillovers. The emphasis was mostly on transfer of technology from MNEs to their SME suppliers and customers, although it was also agreed the MNEs might also acquire the appropriate technology from local SMEs, and possibly eventually acquire the SME firms themselves as well (Acs and Preston 1997).

The final issue is the SME role in investment and the connection between SMEs and FDI. SMEs may advance as multinationals either through their own speculations or because of the arrangement of unions. The questions of why SMEs go abroad, how they do it, and what the impacts of this action are examined carefully (Acs and Preston 1997).

We start by inspecting the technological premise of SMEs. In spite of the fact that, in total, SMEs save on R&D more than bigger firms, they produce twice the same number of developments on a per employee premise (Acs and Audretsch 1990). In 1993 United States, SMEs received 3.8 percent of federal R&D dollars and performed 14.5 percent of company funded industrial R&D (Gewehr 1996). In 1991, SMEs received 40 percent of all domestic utility patents granted in the United States

(U.S. Patent and Trademark Office 1996). The important role of property rights in capitalist economies is getting progressively apparent. Societies have to protect innovators' property rights to make profit from their innovations (Acs and Preston 1997).

The new product, process, and so on are mostly owned by the firm, not the inventor from employees. This reduces creative employees' incentives to innovate for the company. As there is no obvious property rights in bigger corporations, perverse incentives for both managers and employees are being created (Acs and Preston 1997). Contrary to innovative employees in large firms, free innovators can hold clear property rights, can have every incentive to undertake original innovations, and can be hugely free of red tape. Thus, it is argued that SMEs are better at developing original innovations because they protect innovators' property rights in a better way (Acs and Preston 1997).

The conference concluded that international diffusion of new innovations is crucial for continuing the improvement of global economic welfare. In the dissemination cycle, SMEs face two genuine difficulties: property right insurance and barriers to entry. If the rate of creative destruction is indeed too low, public policies should aim to increase the creation and international diffusion of innovations by SMEs. It was suggested that policies should aim to reduce the costs in international expansion for SME. Policies should aim to reduce the private market costs incurred for the protection of property rights, to reduce entry barriers, and to reduce transaction costs (Acs and Preston 1997).

Conclusion

To sum up, SME internationalization has become recently a highly discussed topic in the literature of business modernization. Although the internationalization argument is not a new topic for western business investors, developing countries nowadays are striving for hunting the chance to position themselves in the global market. This chapter has evaluated the appropriate strategies of economic activities to be adopted for expanding into the global market as well as the future internationalization prospects related to the high-tech industry. FDIs are mostly carried by large firms due to the large capital needed to finance the required resources. Hence, exporting and alliances are the best strategic options for start-up businesses. Governments from all over the world have scrutinized the effect of SMEs in local economies. Therefore, they started launching motivational programs to encourage leading entrepreneurship economic growth. Those motivational programs include capital fund, educational programs, business studies, and so on.

CHAPTER 3

The Importance of SMEs on Developing Countries

Introduction

The aim of the chapter is to explore the importance of the SME sector in developing countries. From the results of the study, it was observed that SMEs are essential to economy development. The author used qualitative research methods to conduct secondary research on the topic. Several academic journals as well as published online papers and books were used to achieve a high level of understanding and exploration of the topic. This chapter is based on surveying the literature review and establishing a base for exploring the importance of the SME sector in developing countries. The hypotheses presented here are tested, and the findings are presented. The presented findings revealed that SMEs are key players in ending developing economy problems such as poverty, unemployment, and so on, but this cannot be achieved without government support to SMEs and their protection from developing economy problems like inflation, black market, and so on.

The Concept of SMEs

SMEs contribute a lot to the global economy. For example, 99 percent of enterprises in the European Union (EU) are SMEs, and they provide almost 55 percent of private sector employment (OECD 2004). Unlike large firms and organizations, SMEs have great capability of quick adaptation, which makes them less affected by economic crises. This is exactly why they are seen as the main actors in the development of emerging and developing countries. Because SMEs are flexible and can cope with hard conditions, they are an inspiration for innovation, especially in emerging and developing countries. As stated by the World Bank, formal SMEs contribute up to 60 percent of total employment and up to 40 percent of national income (GDP) in developing economies. Moreover, the World Bank also estimates that in the next 15 years, four out of five jobs will be generated by SMEs in emerging economies and developing countries, mainly in Asia and Sub-Saharan Africa. Hence, nowadays, governments in developing countries are initiating different programs to strengthen SMEs and support their future.

However, SMEs' financial status is often their major weakness. SMEs are usually working on low budget; hence, they will always face obstacles in obtaining sufficient capital for operation and growth. Dalberg Global Development Advisors report that SMEs' role in the private sector growth rate is often too low because SME growth in developing economies is often slowed down due to the difficulty to obtain financial capital. Moreover, they argue that local financial systems do not sufficiently cater for the needs of SMEs.

SMEs have proven to be the backbone that supports the economy of many countries—whether it is a country with high income economy, emerging economy, or even developing economy. For instance, in the OECD economies, SMEs represent over 95 percent of firms, 60 to 70 percent of employment, and 55 percent of GDP. In the case of emerging and developing economies, the situation is not very different. For instance, in Morocco, 93 percent of firms are SMEs and account for 38 percent of production, 33 percent of investment, 30 percent of exports, and 46 percent of employment. Similarly, in Bangladesh, enterprises of less than 100 employees account for 99 percent of all firms and 58 percent of employment. Likewise, in Ecuador, 99 percent of all private companies have less than 50 employees and account for 55 percent of employment. It is because of their efficient operations, innovative leadership, and endurance to surrounding changes that supporting SMEs have proven to be one of the best strategies to support the growth and development of the economy.

However, till this moment and after it has been proven that well-managed and healthy SMEs can be effective to both citizens and governments, SMEs in most of the emerging and developing countries still face many constrains (Davidson 2004). Examples of these constraints are technological backwardness, lack of human resource skills, weak management systems and entrepreneurial capabilities, unavailability of appropriate and timely information, insufficient use of information technology, and poor product quality. As a result, there exists a low level of performance. We hypothesized that if SMEs in developing countries were given the right access to funds and got the chance to work in a formal way under the umbrella of facilitated rules, taxes and regulation, SMEs would help end many of the largest problems of undeveloped economy, for example, black market, unemployment, shortage of resources, poor infrastructure, poverty, foreign trade, and foreign currency rates in the case of inflation.

Table 3.1 Criteria set in 2005 for the definition of SMEs by the EU (Keskøn, entürk, Sungur, and Kørøø 2010)

SME Category	Employment	Turnover (Million €)	Balance Sheet (Million €)
Medium	250	501	43
Small	50	10	10
Micro	10	2	2

SME's definition according to the EU is the micro, small, and medium enterprises (MSMEs) that meet the criteria as shown in Table 3.1:

SMEs differ from large-scale enterprises in almost everything, and like everything in this world, they have their advantages and disadvantages. Advantages are, for example, being more efficient, coping up with economic crises, and having a competitive structure. As for disadvantages, examples are having lower level of profitability, intense employment, low-level employment, and lack of experts. Differences between SMEs and large enterprises are clarified in Table 3.2.

Table 3.2 Comparison of small and large firms (Xhepa 2006)

	SMEs	Large enterprises
Marketing	Re-active marketing	Proactive marketing
Management	Lack of bureaucracy, more dynamcy, quick response to new opportunities, more willingness to accept risk	Professional managers that control complex organizations to establish corporate strategies
Communications	Efficient and informal internal communication networks, lack of time or resources to identify and use important external sources	Heavy internal communication that often leads to slow reaction to external threats/ opportunities, better ability to fund important external sources
Qualified technical manpower	Frequent lack of suitably qualified technical specialists, inability often to support a formal R&D effort	Ability to attract highly skilled technical specialists, ability to support a large R&D scale
Finance	Great difficulty in attracting capital, especially risk capital, innovation can represent a financial risk	Ability to borrow on capital market, ability to spread risk over a portfolio of projects
The system approach	Inability to offer integrated product lines or systems	Ability to offer a range of complementary products
Economies of scale	Scale economies, in some areas, form entry barriers to small firms	Ability to gain scale economies in R&D, production, and marketing
Growth	Possibility of experiencing difficulty in acquiring resources necessary for rapid growth	Ability to finance expansion of production and fund growth via diversification and acquisition
Government regulations	No ability often to cope with complex regulations, costs of compliance unit in small firms often high	Ability to fund legal services to cope with complex regulatory requirements

It is proven that regardless of whether it is a developed or developing country, SMEs play an important role in the overall growth of economy and contribute a lot to countries having low level of investment by offering many socio-economic benefits (Gamage 2003). However, the share of SMEs differs according to the surrounding economic status. As shown in Table 3.3, the share of SMEs in the economy differs globally from one group of countries to another.

Table 3.3 Share of SMEs in global economy (Lukács 2005)

EU	99% of enterprises in the EU are defined as SMEs and employ around 75 million. On average, each SME provides employment for 4 people, including the owner/manager and the average turnover is € 500,000.
OECD countries	Over 95% of enterprises in most of OECD countries are SMEs, and it generates over 50% of private sector employment. Moreover, most OECD governments promote and develop SMEs with policies and programs like tax breaks or reducing interest loans for starting new businesses in rural areas.
Latin America	Around 80–90% of enterprises are micro, and the governments have vastly reduced bureaucratic obstacles to ensure SME needs are attended to swiftly. These businesses flourished, especially in Brazil and Mexico.
Asia	The world's best performing economies, notably Taiwan and Hong Kong, are heavily based on small enterprises. In addition, SMEs contribute 81% to employment in Japan, where on average, SMEs employ 9 staff as opposed to 4 in the EU.
South Africa	It is estimated that 60% of the share of employment is located in SMEs while the sector generated about 40% of output.

Struggles of SMEs in Emerging Economy and Developing Countries

Despite the initiatives done by governments to support SMEs and boost their growth, there is still a gap in financing, and there is scope for government interventions to close this gap and enhance SMEs' operating environment (Bouri, Breij, Diop, Kempner, Klinger, and Stevenson 2011). SMEs are still struggling to reach their economic potential because of issues like informality and absence of well-established lending system (Bouri et al. 2011). Even though SMEs are a strong weapon to fight poverty and unemployment, and it is a fact that SMEs are vital to emerging economy and developing countries, yet governments still do not act against the five most significant obstacles that threaten SMEs. Those five obstacles are access to finance, tax rate, competition, electricity, and political factors.

Among those five obstacles, access to finance appears to be the biggest barrier (Wang 2016).

Financing of SMEs in Emerging Economy and Developing Countries and Its Effect on Probability and Performance

According to the HFC Bank (2004), SMEs in some of the developing countries, like Ghana, tend to have limited access to credit. It was also revealed in a recent report of the Central Bank of Egypt that only 8 percent of small businesses in Egypt have bank loans. In Jordan, the share of credit to SMEs declined from 11 to 8.5 percent of the total credit available to the private sector. It was proven that SMEs are 23.1 percentage more likely to distinguish access to finance as the biggest obstacles to their growth than large firms (Wang 2016). Surveys showed that smaller firms experience more severe financing problems than larger firms. How severe is access to finance as an obstacle to the current operation of the firm? The answer of this question mainly depends on the firm size (Wang 2016). As elaborated in the following table, internal funds are the main source of financing for SMEs. It is shown that 54.53 percent of SMEs did not need loan for financing their business. And among SMEs that need financing, it is evident that 14.35 percent suffer from high interests and 9.61 percent suffer from complexity of application procedures.

With financing being a major constraint facing SMEs, it has direct effect on productivity and profitability. By doing meta-analysis on developing countries, Kersten, Harms, Liket, and Maas (2017) found that SMEs finance programs have a positive and significant impact on performance key indicators, such as capital investment and employment, yet they have an insignificant effect on profitability and wages. Beck and Demirguç-Kunt (2006) warn that access to financing is not the only thing that affects performance but also the type of finance, especially for SMEs in developing countries. They suggest that out-of-the-box lending strategies, such as factoring, credit-scoring, and leasing, are better alternatives to traditional debt financing because of the absence of developed institutions and the presence of weak business environment like that of emerging and developing countries.

Table 3.4 Reasons for not applying for a loan (Wang 2016)

Main reason for not applying for new loans or new lines of credit	Percent
Don't know	1.17
Refuse to answer	0.06
No response	0.01
Still in process	1.42
Skip	0.01
No need for a loan	54.53
Application procedures for loans are complex	9.61
Interest rates are not favorable	14.35
Collateral requirements are too high	6.95
Size of loan or maturity are insufficient	1.85
It is necessary to make informal payments	3.07
Did not think it would be approved	6.24
Other	0.73
Total	100

Infrastructure in Emerging Economy and Developing Countries and Its Effect on SMEs' Probability and Performance

Lack of infrastructure can have a negative impact on SME performance and profitability. This is particularly accurate in cases of emerging economies and developing countries where bad infrastructures—like electricity, water, telecommunication, and so on—can burden SME extra cost to obtain such services. In addition, such bad conditions result in bad working environments affecting performance. All of this hampers SME growth (Mambula 2002). In a case study, Anwar (2010) proves how governments in collaboration with local SMEs came up with solutions that better infrastructure. This process generated social benefits for the entire industrial district. Similarly, Akuru and Okoro (2014) highlight that SME villages or clusters can be built in Nigeria to promote industrial activities. Such strategic development would enable the provision of basic infrastructures such as the electricity needed for spin-offs as well as operations more affordably. This is particularly important in the case of developing economies where infrastructure may be undeveloped or underdeveloped. Lack or decay of infrastructure can lead to the failure of SMEs (Ndiaye, Razak, Nagayev, and Ng 2018).

Informality of SMEs in Emerging Economy and Developing Countries and Its Effect on Profitability and Performance

In developing countries, informal firms get the lion share. Most of the people live on what is called *informal economy*. It makes up a large portion of overall employment and economic activities. As found by La Porta and Shleifer (2008), informal SMEs are extremely unproductive when compared to formal SMEs. Even though informal SMEs can be a great source of employment, informality can impact productivity negatively. Thus, the formalization of SMEs is often associated with better performance. The same thing was also proven by Rand and Torm (2012) when they studied the effects of formalization on firm-level outcomes in SMEs in Vietnam. The results proved that formalization leads to an increase in firm gross profits and investment as well as in the empowerment of workers. However, they found no evidence that formalizing leads to a higher share of wages in the total value added.

Regulation and Taxes of SMEs in Emerging Economy and Developing Countries and Its Effect on Profitability and Performance

Regulation and taxes can work in favor of SMEs or against them. It can be used to create a good business environment that allows SMEs to grow and expand, or it can have a negative impact on profitability and performance. All depends on how it is used, and how it allows and gives opportunity to new businesses or SMEs. Klapper, Laeven, and Rajan (2006) used a database of developed and developing European countries and found that costly regulations ease the creation of new industries. The study concluded that poor business environments might affect SME performance because restrictions and market imperfections dampen competition and slow firm growth. Troilo (2011) concluded that poor performance among SMEs in emerging economies is an effect of corruption and noncompetitive banking. The study also stated that the persistence of noncompetitive banking is a result of government regulatory choice in restricting the entry of foreign banks.

SMEs Profitability and Performance in Developing Economy Under the Shadow of Inflation

Inflation influences demand, interest rates, exchange rates, unemployment, and consumption. Hence, it directly impacts the growth of SMEs because all these factors can affect sales, revenues, and market potential of SMEs (The Economist 2009). It also impacts the market potential not only growth opportunities of SMEs. The findings show that economic matters such as sustained inflation suppresses entrepreneurial activities, especially the small businesses (Thompson Agyapong, Mmieh, and Mordi 2018). The results reveal that persistent inflation is one of the major constraints affecting the activities and growth of businesses across all sectors and industries. It results in high production costs, lower profits, and often zero profits, hence putting all SMEs that operate in inflamed economy under the risk of failure.

SMEs Role in Ending Economic Problems in Developing Countries

As noted in the research conducted by Keskøn et al. (2010), developing countries are interested in SMEs for two main reasons. The first is that SME development is an effective anti-poverty program. The second is that SME development is one of the best inspirations for innovation and sustainable growth. Several studies were conducted on the importance of SMEs to economy development in developing countries. According to Kachembere (2011), SMEs play a vital role in economic growth and sustainable development because economic growth goes hand in hand with poverty reduction and social growth. Therefore, SMEs are considered vital for poverty reduction and social growth as well as economic growth, which, in turn, can put an end to unemployment, inflation, black market, corruption, low standard of education, and many other economic and social problems. That is why, most of the now developed countries have depended on the growing of the SME sector to solve economic and social problems.

Governments' Efforts in Supporting SMEs

Different initiatives were taken by governments and policy makers to solve SMEs major problem, that is, financing. Like, for example, the New Ventures Investor Forums, which are forums that bring together financial and business committees to provide support to SMEs. Moreover, governments try to offer other nonfinancial solutions like mentoring and management trainings to be provided to SME owners and managers (Pandya 2012). Many governments have put into action plans to support SMEs, which included financial aspects like forums and programs that include facilitated loans and bank services. As mentioned, governments also try developing entrepreneurs and managers through mentoring programs and training to meet the SMEs' management and leadership needs. Unfortunately, though, these efforts are not enough because SME problems fall beyond financing and managers' development. SMEs need support in many aspects like marketing, research and development (R&D), technology, human resources (HR), governance, and so on.

In fact, marketing has been recognized as one of the biggest obstacles facing SME operations and one of the most essential elements for business survival (Simpson and Taylor 2002). In addition, globalization got SMEs pressured, especially in the field of manufacturing (Raymond and St-Pierre 2004). Therefore, it is essential for developing countries to support R&D in order to gain competitive advantage over foreign competitors. Despite globalization, most SMEs in developing countries work with the traditional approach, resulting in low productivity, quality, and locality, which is why the usage of latest technology and having the maximum utility of machinery would positively affect production.

Theoretical Frameworks

Recent studies confirmed that economic growth is directly linked to the development of SMEs within the country. As noted by various researchers like Beck (2005) and Ardic, Mylenko, and Saltane (2011), there is a direct relation between the size of the SME sector and economic growth. The majority of employment opportunities are only generated through the growth of the SME sector. It is worth highlighting, though, that despite the proven influence of SMEs on developing economies, SMEs still need support to grow and overcome their obstacles. It is proven in many studies that there is no standard model for SMEs as it is a highly adaptive enterprise that differs according to its environment. However, we can say that there are main areas where most SMEs need support. According to Ricupero, Warner, Narain, Güttler, Kasekende, Zouari, Kloeppinger-Todd, Narasimham, Bays, and Dunsby (2001), SMEs mainly need support during the startup phase so that they can have the chance to grow and be visible in the local economy and political prosses, and this can only be done through government support. According to Curran, Rutherfoord, and Smith (2000), small business owners tend to be detached from local economic initiatives. This appears to be due to historical trends that have reduced the role of small business in local political processes (Smith 2000). Even though it is observed that the role of SMEs is increasing significantly in respective national economies, SMEs are generally underrepresented in world trade (OECD 2005). Therefore, measures are required to be taken to make its share significant.

Furthermore, in order to activate the magic of SMEs, which will save the economy of developing countries through contributing to the national income, employment, poverty reduction and export revenues, SMEs need to address some challenges (OECD 2004). One of these challenges is how the enterprise is going to expand in the shadow of establishing new innovative firms every day. Therefore, SMEs must be competitive and productive. In fact, they must reach a certain level of competitiveness that enables them to integrate through trades and investments, like exports and internationalization.

In conclusion, there are different definitions of SMEs in different countries, and there is no standard business model for them. SMEs have an important role in terms of economic growth, poverty reduction, social growth, and sustainability. SMEs have gained popularity, especially in developing economies, because of their flexibility and ability to adapt fast and not being affect by economic crises. In addition, SMEs are the vital actors that represent entrepreneurship, innovation, and competitiveness. That is why governments need to exert efforts to help and support SMEs to overcome obstacles like finances and business continuity and also to encourage the formation of formal SMEs.

Conclusion

It is found that SMEs have a direct impact on economic and social development depending on government support for SMEs in the country. Thus, it should be extremely important for the governments of developing countries to support SMEs in all required aspects and all business stages. Based on the findings of the study, the following is recommended:

- Formulating different action plans to specifically meet the needs of SMEs in each phase (start-up phase/development phase/business-continuity phase) in order to reduce their early failure and guarantee continuous development.
- Facilitating the loan process for SMEs through providing low interest rate, simple application procedure, and flexible collateral requirements. Facilitating other ways of financing SMEs, like leasing, angel investors, partnership investing, and so on.
- Developing out-of-the-box ideas that act as win–win for economy development and SMEs. For example, creating milestones for SMEs, and when they reach them, the enterprise gets support from the government. This support could be in the form of interest-free loans, tax free consultation services for a certain period of time, and so on. The milestones could be having a certain employment rate, gender equality in employment opportunities, doing community services (providing low-priced goods to the poor, giving opportunities to the youth as interns, etc.), and so on.

- Providing SMEs with consultation services regarding all aspects—not only the financial aspect but also the technological, HR, and strategy aspects as well as the organizational aspect and so on.
- Developing programs for SMEs that are about to fail to provide guidance and offer solutions like merging with other SMEs or increasing cash flow, and so on.
- Protecting SMEs from developing economy obstacles. For example, in the case of black market, governments are to provide SMEs with the needed material or foreign currency, and so on.

CHAPTER 4

International Best Practice SME Promotion Agencies

Introduction

The small size of SMEs, the challenge of real exchange rate, limited access to finance, bureaucratic procedures in setup, poor infrastructures, poor skilled manpower, globalization, and trade liberalization between countries put more challenges before SMEs. Removing these obstacles would increase SME development, which in turn would grow economic capacity and help decrease unemployment.

SME development requires the ability of governments to endorse cross-cutting strategies for macroeconomic policies. This can be done through simplified legal and regulatory framework, good governance, accessible finance, suitable infrastructures, supportive education, sufficiently healthy and flexible skilled labor, enhanced partnership between stakeholders in the private and governmental sectors, directing SMEs to new areas of investment, opening markets for producing products and services locally and regionally, increasing financial support, and so on.

SMEs are a major source of job creation. Their capability to support economic strategies that would realize quick and sustainable growth leads us to study how to promote and support SMEs through promotion agencies.

Strengthening SME Competitiveness in Transition and Developing Countries

Introducing new products with product combinations and innovation is a driving force for growth and expansion of SMEs that continuously give them competitive advantage to sustain and grow in health and wealth conditions. Emphasis has changed to the importance of achieving international competitiveness, to programs that encourage business growth, and to support for technology based businesses. The creation of an enterprise culture within society has started to gain in importance. Peace and stability are a key requirement for the development of SMEs and for attracting foreign investment. Studies show that war and crime are main deterrents of private investment, in particular for foreign investors. Stability in legislation and laws are also key points to secure and attract foreign investment to start-up SMEs. The ability of governments to implement sound macroeconomic policies and the capability of stakeholders to develop conducive microeconomic business environments are also major factors that have significant impact on the sustainability of SMEs. Dialogue and partnerships between stakeholders (in the public and private sectors and civil society) are essential. Enhancing women's ability to participate in SME development should be taken into account at every stage and level.

SMEs Cut Across Sectors

Improving SME competitiveness requires policies that act on the economic, political, and social institutions within the country. An SME development strategy has to bring to the forefront the challenges that SMEs face due to size effects and should address the deficiencies. There is a need for a cross-cutting SME strategy embedded in the national development framework in institutional and organizational structures with a view to enhancing SME competitiveness.

Development of Human and Natural Resources

Empirical studies show that human capital is a significant determinant of growth. The ability of SMEs to adjust to the competitive pressures that come with trade liberalization and globalization very much depends on the level of skills that are available within transition and developing economies. Particularly, the least developing countries are investing significantly in their education (mainly basic) and training systems. Education and training systems have the opportunity to influence the level of entrepreneurial activity in transition and developing economies where new and innovative enterprise creation is a priority.

Supporting Infrastructure

Infrastructure investments, such as those in transport, telecommunications, energy, water and sanitation, can enhance SME/private sector activity and ability to access local, regional, and global markets. Furthermore, the quality of available infrastructure has a significant influence on SME competitiveness. It is important that infrastructure services reach all segments of society such as the poorest and rural areas in order to enable SMEs of different sizes, and from all areas, to participate in economic activity. Infrastructure affects all sizes of business: power cuts, roads swept away by floods, and so on. Absence of port and railway facilities affect SMEs as well as large-scale businesses. However, incomplete or under-maintained infrastructure particularly affects the livelihoods of the rural poor in developing and transition countries since large proportions of rural poor regions are involved in agriculture and agro-processing, including fisheries. Low-quality infrastructure prevents the commercialization of production based on rural resources. Additionally, poor infrastructure results in low levels of entrepreneurial activity in rural areas and large-scale rural to urban migration, thereby putting pressure on urban infrastructure, employment in urban areas, and so on. Starting around 1970s, industrial estates for SMEs have been employed as an instrument for the development of depressed regions in a large number of developing countries.

Supporting SME Export Development

Globalization has created new opportunities for SMEs. Progressive globalization over the last two decades or so has created a new international environment for SME exports from developing countries. The process of world economic integration has involved broadening and deepening of inter-relationships between international trade and foreign investment flows. Several influences at the macroeconomic level, sound government policies, and the ability to stabilize a competitive real exchange rate are cornerstones of promoting exports. A competitive real exchange rate provides an incentive for exports. Moreover, an outward-oriented, market-friendly trade regime, which emphasizes the dismantling of import controls and tariffs (permitting access to inputs at world prices) and streamlined bureaucratic procedures (i.e., export and import procedures, modern customs administration, and efficient value added tax administration), will facilitate exports, including from SMEs. Developing capacity-building programs that include supply chain and cluster initiatives, which recognize the potential for developing tiers of suppliers to maximize trickle down effects, including micro enterprises as lower-tier supplies, is essential.

Improving Aid Effectiveness

SME development has a long history of evolution in almost all donor countries. Implementation of an SME development strategy needs the participation and collaboration of numerous stakeholders. Getting the fundamentals right in the legal, regulatory, and administrative frameworks has the greatest impact on SME development in most contexts. The SME field is wide and experiences are many. These considerations have the potential to introduce confusion on the part of partners—with different donors giving noncomplementary, at times, conflicting advice—and can result in disconnected interventions. Donor coordination is crucial to improve the efficiency and effectiveness of resources both on partner and donor sides. Such coordination should be based on joint analytical work toward assessing and prioritizing needs. Without proper administrative capacities, especially at local levels where entrepreneurs have their contact with improved frameworks, it would be difficult to achieve the intended results.

Conclusion

SME development cuts across sectors, involves multiple stakeholders, and necessitates concerted actions by the public and private sector with a view to removing supply-side constraints to trade and investment. It requires firms to build up their competitive advantages. Improving the investment climate for SMEs and strengthening their capacities to respond to trade and investment opportunities do strengthen the economic performance of SMEs, and this, in turn, has a positive impact on growth and poverty reduction.

CHAPTER 5

SME Policy Index

Introduction

Government policies have a major impact on private entrepreneurship in the early stage, and policies are related to many areas such as taxes, public procurement, licenses, and permits. There are two areas of government policy: taxes and government support.

Egypt achieved an average of 4.2 close to the global average of 4.3, and this number indicates little improvement from the past. Through examination, government policies that favor new companies have emerged, in general, through regulatory reforms, supporting for new programs, amending some investment laws in Egypt, and launching programs to support entrepreneurship.

Government Entrepreneurship Programs

Government support programs play an important role for entrepreneurship, especially in disadvantaged and marginalized societies. Egypt score is 3.3 in this program, compared with the global average of 4.3. Government programs in Egypt scored low on availability, accessibility, and effectiveness.

Entrepreneurship Education

With regard to providing basic business education on how to start and run a business in areas such as marketing, finance, and strategic operations, Egypt ranks lower than all countries in school education and university education. Egypt score is 3.4 in entrepreneurial education, compared with the global average of 4.8. Currently, there are ambitious initiatives by the government to introduce educational reforms.

Research and Development Transfer

The ability to transfer technology from universities and research centers in the industry is absolutely necessary to move from an efficient economy to an innovation-based one. Egypt score is 2.9, compared with the global average of 3.9.

The link between the industry and universities and researches is very low, which highlights the problem of separation between research, the industry, and technology transfer.

Commercial and Legal Infrastructure

Commercial and legal infrastructure highlights the ability of a new and growing firm to access legal, accounting, banking, and consulting services as well. Egypt score is 4, compared to the global average of 4.9. In most of the areas surveyed, grades are still close to the past two years for major legal reforms taking place in investment laws and industrial licenses.

Internal Market Dynamics

This is the internal market dynamics on the new company ability to enter, compete, and grow in a specific economy. There are two areas for market dynamics:

- The level of change in the market
- Market entry regulations

Egypt score is 5.8, compared to the global average of 5.1.

Physical Infrastructure

Physical infrastructure describes the ease of access to physical resources. Physical infrastructure in Egypt is the strongest area among the entrepreneurship framework conditions. The availability of physical infrastructure in Egypt regularly increased over the past five years. especially with regard to roads, utilities, and water. Egypt score is 6, compared to the global average of 6.5.

Cultural and Social Norms

Cultural and social norms describe the extent to which culture encourages or allows actions or activities leading to new businesses. Egypt score is 4, compared to the global average of average 4.8. In general, there is a trend to support the key features of entrepreneurship such as risk, creativity, and innovation.

Experts' Views and Recommendations

Based on expert recommendations, we are in urgent need of:

(a) Reducing government bureaucracy and red tape, which remains a major obstacle for start-ups, as well as organizing reforms and simplifying laws related to licenses, permits, and tax collection
(b) Obtaining financing, which is still a priority, both for start-up companies driven by innovation or for investors
(c) Teaching entrepreneurship at all levels and promoting a culture of entrepreneurship
(d) Allowing space for the experiment to be more able to adapt to organizational matters

Key Factors Constraining Entrepreneurship in Egypt

1. Limited access to financing
2. The lack of sufficient number of investors and the absence of financing opportunities for public subscription
3. Lack of national support in the science based on high-tech market
4. Governmental and bureaucratic regulations and laws due to the lack of a comprehensive political vision in the relevant areas, such as education and taxes, and the lack of a stable judicial system

5. Bureaucracy and inefficiency in legal work with the government
6. Corruption and a bad legal system
7. Weakness and absence of the ecosystem for entrepreneurship outside Cairo and Alexandria
8. Lack of access to rapid education, especially in the skills that are needed to run a business—in other words, education for entrepreneurship by the government
9. The attitude of the government and political decision makers toward sabotage is often extremely negative
10. The absence of appropriate channels for competitive competition for start-ups
11. Lack of a good cultural environment and lack of access to new knowledge or exposure to new ways of doing business
12. Government regulations, especially bankruptcy law
13. Challenges related to supply chain management and logistic services for production to the global market

Key Factors Fostering Entrepreneurship in Egypt

1. Good infrastructure
2. A high percentage of community supporters and ecosystem developers, which leads to availability of meeting spaces and exchange of ideas
3. Several capacity-building initiatives in the field of entrepreneurship provided by the government
4. Multiple market failures, which lead to strong demand for products and services
5. The vital role played by a group of investors and businessmen in supporting and guiding start-ups
6. Access to world-class development opportunities sponsored by the government
7. Appointment of an entity by the government to collect all services for entrepreneurs
8. The existence of good training programs by community organizations at schools and universities
9. Universities and research centers

10. The presence of a vibrant ecosystem in Cairo with a lot of investment and support

11. Culture and traditions of family business and social ability

12. Currency devaluation providing opportunity for export to markets

13. The promotion of entrepreneurship as a career path by the increasing number of youth and the presence of role models for young entrepreneurs

14. The existence of some governmental initiatives to supporting entrepreneurs, such as the Central Bank initiative

15. The government growing interest in entrepreneurship resulting in the new investment law

16. The IT sector providing promises and an open market in entrepreneurship

Key Recommendations to Support Entrepreneurship in Egypt

1. The inclusion of entrepreneurship in the education, especially at universities and schools in Egypt

2. The expansion of science parks outside Cairo

3. Working on developing the spirit of initiative and risk for the youth and society as a whole

4. Ensuring a more coherent government policy to support project initiatives and enable better access to financing

5. More government participation and support

6. Establishing appropriate government support mechanisms for technology innovation

7. Clear industry mapping

8. Working to reform financial policies and their stability in the market, especially the interest and exchange rates

9. Encouraging the government in legal ways for companies that are three years old or less

10. Government support for participation and financing, with adequate supply programs without monopoly, thus helping companies generate opportunities

11. Changing the culture through media awareness and highlighting success stories of young entrepreneurs

12. Encouraging and educating students about entrepreneurship at primary and secondary education and supporting innovation in educational curricula

13. Providing more flexible legislation and regulations to support entrepreneurial activity

14. Providing government subsidies to encourage companies to start

15. Ensuring small tax exemptions for new start-ups

Recommendations for Policy and Practice

The entrepreneurial system in Egypt has grown in the past three years, creating a positive atmosphere as a result of new programs and political reforms, and as a result of that, project organization indicators in Egypt have improved.

As a result, we list some recommendations for policy and practice as follows:

1. Positioning Egypt as a Regional Hub for Entrepreneurship and Innovation

Egypt has the ability to become a regional center for establishing innovative technology companies, and these types of companies operate as comprehensive growth platforms. Egypt has influencing factors for such a strategy from a strong talent pool and a large market.

First: Improving access to project financing—in particular venture capital funds

Second: Providing incentives to retain technical means and managerial talents and working on developing them

2. Expanding Entrepreneurial Education and Awareness Among Youth

The government is implementing radical reforms in the Egyptian education system, but this takes time to translate into actual impact among youth.

There are two specific areas that need focusing on:

First: Building trust between youth and young professionals to start their own business

Second: Providing the foundational knowledge of business management, with a focus on the needs of small and medium-sized companies

3. **Unleashing the Power of Youth Entrepreneurship for Inclusive Growth and Job Creation**

Most of the narrative around entrepreneurship is focused on tech start-ups, and they ignore the small and medium companies that provide the social and economic basis and work to create job opportunities, although they can be easily accelerated for faster growth and more productivity. Significant progress has been made in obtaining financing for SMEs. In addition, major reforms have been implemented in the areas of investment laws and industrial licensing requirements, but dealing with 12 government agencies drains resources and energy for microenterprises and impedes growth.

4. **Strengthening the Entrepreneurship Ecosystem Through Programs and Policies**

The emerging entrepreneurship ecosystem in Egypt is a promising system and can have a major impact on economic growth. Many indicators confirm this in the light of the improvements in the areas of obtaining financing, government policies, and easier access to markets.

On the government side, there are many organizational reforms and support programs that have been implemented over the past three years, especially in the areas of investment and corporate and bankruptcy laws.

CHAPTER 6

Small and Medium-Sized Enterprises (SMEs) and Sustainable Development Goals (SDGs)

Introduction

In September 2015, World Leaders adopted a sustainable development plan for 2030, and in early 2017, they set 17 goals for sustainable development, which will officially come into effect over the next 15 years. All countries set their sights on those new goals and mobilize efforts to overcome all shapes of poverty and forester well-being. They agree that ending poverty must go hand in hand with all strategies that could help in increasing economic growth and meeting a wide range of social needs, including educational needs, health insurance, social protection, and new job opportunities. At the same time, they should address change impacts on the climate and work for environmental protection. Governments should take the lead and establish national frameworks for the achievement of those goals.

The goals can be summarized as follows: overcoming poverty everywhere, achieving food security, ending hunger, guaranteeing healthy lives for all at all ages, providing sustainable and modern energy for all, offering good education for all, equality, offering sustainable water and sanitation supply for all, limiting external and internal conflicts in all countries, making safe cities, ensuring sustainable patterns of production and consumption, increasing employment opportunities, increasing economic growth rate, developing all marine resources, fostering peaceful societies, reducing the impact of climate change, taking fast actions, and so on.

Studies point out that small and medium enterprises (SMEs) account for the majority of private sector business and economic activity in both developed and developing countries. Hence, it is necessary to go through and further understand the importance and potential contribution to sustainable development goals (SDGs). Those goals aim to boost the access to small-scale businesses and other enterprises, especially in the newly developing countries.

Referring to the World Bank and the OECD, many reasons could explain how SME/MSME development is playing a critical role for achieving SDGs:

MSMEs play a crucial role in most of local economies, especially in developing countries as formal MSMEs may cover up to 45 percent of the total employment needs and up to 33 percent of gross domestic product (GDP) in emerging market economies. These figures would be significantly increased if informal MSMEs were included. MSMEs are major creators of new opportunities for employment. For example, in emerging markets, four out of five new opportunities of the formal sector were created by MSMEs, which is almost 90 percent of total opportunities. The World Bank reported that 600 million new opportunities will be required in the next 15 years to absorb the highly growing global workforce, mainly in Asian countries and Sub-Saharan Africa.

MSMEs are significantly vital in reducing poverty, especially in countryside areas and between women and others disadvantaged groups. Because of their role and place in local economies, MSMEs are helping to meet SDGs, mostly economic related goals. These goals include promoting inclusive and sustainable economic growth rate, increasing job opportunities and decent work, especially for the poor, advancing sustainable industrialization and innovation, and creating a good push for a higher quality of life, better education level, and good health for all. Given that MSMEs take part in achieving most of the economic related goals of SDGs, the Action Agenda of Addis-Ababa on Financing for Development highlighted the vital role of MSMEs with regard to providing job opportunities and innovation for sustainable development in developing countries. That agenda also encouraged national governments, financial institutions, and development banks to give support for MSME growth by providing a conducive regulatory framework, innovative financial solutions, and systematic entrepreneurship training programs.

For example, in Singapore, there are more than 100,000 SMEs, representing 70 percent of the total SMEs in the country that use business support programs organized by governmental agencies and centers for enterprise developing. It is becoming increasingly necessary for governments to provide all needed resources, services, and funds for the worthy SMEs and start-ups. It is equally important to provide these MSMEs and start-ups with opportunities to share and transfer their knowledge across the business ecosystem with other investors, research centers, and stakeholders through a platform.

One of the multi aspects of MSME development is the social entrepreneurship concept. Solving most environmental and social challenges using business is gaining momentum in west and east African countries, especially in agriculture and telecommunication problems. However, despite the rise in global commitment to their growth, SMEs are still facing many challenges such as the lack of funds, limited access to finances, lack of training and knowledge, particularly regarding business development aspects, and insufficiency of strategic management skills.

Given the potential of MSMEs for SDGs, there is a need for more systematic changes in policies and in the ways of operation at financial markets and institutions. This would be able to reduce the challenges MSMEs face in accessing financial resources and encourage the development of informal SMEs to formal ones. This, in turn, would result in additional economic growth and the generation of more job opportunities. The SDG Compass is the way to translate the 17 UN SDGs into management objectives. The SDG Compass mainly highlights large corporations and offers them the framework and methods to transform the SDGs into business. Those implementation methods for SDGs and the framework with goals can meet the criteria of a hands-on and an actionable tool. More attention is paid to other motivators instead of highlighting tangible business impact. Currently, it is not possible to prioritize the topics of greatest interest to European SMEs. There are no tools to link the SDGs to the business operations of SMEs. SMEs lack resources, expertise, and incentives to implement sustainability in their day-to-day management, but their potential contribution to sustainable development is substantial.

While the SME sector makes a significant contribution to the economies of countries, high failure rates in these small businesses and enterprises is a matter of major concern. Studies on small enterprises in various areas of the world show that the most cited problems of small enterprises are related to lack of management, business development, and marketing skills. Brand personality is an innovative marketing potential for SMEs to compete with larger, more established firms more effectively. Thus, building brand personalities could assist in achieving SDGs 8 and 9 by enhancing sustainability and inequality between small, medium, and large-sized enterprises, which will be beneficial to growth in developing countries and in economic productivity.

Conclusion

SDGs will be the most important driving force with regard to laws, directives, and policies for stakeholder and investors in the next 15 years. This will lead to proper allocation of private and public resources to achieve more SDGs—economic related projects—which result in increasing the growth rate of markets. Therefore, markets at the bottom will be closer to those companies with high technologies, thus providing new solutions for most problems. Moreover, integrating business strategies with the SDGs will help companies to overcome the unexpected legal and market changes. Eventually, SDGs compliance will result in reducing legal and other business risks.

CHAPTER 7

Protecting Minority Investors

Introduction

What are minority investors? Minority investors have a minority interest in a company, which is a percentage of ownership that is significant but does not give the holder the right to control the company. What is the meaning of protecting minority investors? The protection of minority investors indicators measure the strength of minority shareholder protection against the misuse by directors of corporate assets for their personal gain. They also measure shareholders' rights, governance safeguards, and corporate transparency requirements that reduce the risk of abuse. Why make a minority investment? Among those hundreds of thousands of privately held companies, many seek new or expanded market opportunities looking for cash for new equipment, and so on. A typical company has essentially three ways to obtain such financing: drawing on internally available funds, financing through external debt, or equity.

The Risks Faced by Minority Investors

The first option for obtaining financing is to source funds internally when the owner or owners get profits from current operations instead of ploughing them back into the business. However, this requires owners with financial reserves and patience sufficient to forego these profits. If the necessary reserves and patience are unavailable, the owners look externally for either debt or equity financing. If the company has a relatively predictable cash flow and assets to pledge, a bank loan can make sense, but if the company has less predictable cash flow and the opportunity has a greater upside potential, equity financing (new investors) can be a preferred option. The company ability to attract such external financing (investors) depends on many factors. One is the investor's perceived risk of not receiving an adequate return within a foreseeable timeframe, either because operational plans fail to meet the objectives (business risk) or the investor's rights are not respected (legal risk).

A new investor can give a business owner the chance to build a new partnership and provide additional liquidity. Majority shareholders would maintain control over most of the company important decisions, while minority investments can often:

- Generate more funds than a leveraged recapitalization
- Help preserve company culture and reputation
- Provide business stability
- Allow expansion
- Bring in shareholders with valuable industry contacts and expertise

The risks minority investors face in privately held companies can be complex and considerable. When unchecked by law or well-crafted shareholder agreements, a dishonest majority investor has substantial opportunities to shape company decisions for their own gain and to the detriment of minority shareholders. For example, a controlling shareholder may redirect resources from a company they own jointly to another that they own fully, thus swindling minority investors of part of the value of their equity stake. Without adequate safeguards that should be in place, majority investors could potentially do so with little transparency or room for minority shareholders to voice their opinions. Furthermore, by investing in companies not traded publicly on a stock market, minority investors have limited options to exit challenging situations.

Potential Challenges Faced by Minority Investors

Minority investors share ownership of a privately held company with individuals who, unless checked by other restraints, have de facto control over the company operations and information. This creates incentives for the controlling investors to divert firm resources from the company as a whole (where sharing is more likely) to other areas (where it is less likely). Some examples abound of controlling investors:

- Refusing to distribute dividends despite profits that would make such distribution reasonable
- Granting unreasonably high salaries, bonuses, and fringe benefits for management positions held by the controlling investors and favored individuals
- Making unreasonably high payments to suppliers of the company that are controlled by the controlling investor or by favored individuals
- Dismissing, without cause, a minority investor from an employment position in the company
- And/or selling all, or nearly all, of the company assets at an inadequate price to a third party controlled by the investor or to favored individuals

In the light of the aforementioned challenges, the term *protecting minority investors* has started to be considered pointedly on corporate governance in privately held companies.

How to Protect Minority Investors? Policies Encouraging Transparency

Minority investors cannot be protected without easy access to corporate information, but this information is only beneficial if it is complete and accurate. Annual audits by internal auditors and licensed external professionals help ensure this.

Doing Business 2020, a World Bank Group flagship publication, addresses transparency for minority investors in a privately held company by inquiring whether the company financial statements must be audited by an external auditor. It is nearly universally accepted that publicly listed companies should perform external audits. It is also nearly universally accepted that financial audits increase investor confidence.

Transparency and Participation Policies That Promote Minority Investor Protection

Doing Business provides policies that protect investors who actively seek to protect their interests. It inquires into three topics that promote informed minority investor participation:

- Must members meet at least once per year?
- Can members representing 10 percent of company capital call for a meeting of members?
- Can members representing 5 percent of company capital put items in a meeting agenda?

These questions point to policies that facilitate investor participation in the limited company. The first two questions focus on factors that ensure controlling members (investors) cannot have the opportunity to meet to discuss matters pertaining to the company. The third ensures that minority members (investors) can have a say in what gets discussed when company members (investors) do meet.

Policies Helping Minority Investors Maintain Initial Agreement

Minority investors typically enjoy their strongest position when negotiating their initial investment. Three issues are considered for helping minority investors maintain initial agreements:

1. Must all members or most members agree to add a new member?
2. Must a member first offers to sell his interest to an existing member before selling it to a nonmember?
3. Does the sale of 51 percent of company assets require member approval?

The first two questions point to legal provisions that give existing minority shareholders a say and right in any changes in the makeup of company membership. This can be very important for smaller companies where members often work closely with each other on behalf of the company, and the right mix of people is important. The third question points to provisions (e.g., a veto over asset sales) that give members a say in a transaction that would likely lead to a substantial change in the company profile. It also allows them to evaluate whether the sale benefits the company. As with rules facilitating minority investor participation, there appears to be few downsides to including the rules here, at least as default ones, in a company law.

Policies to Ensure Minority Investor Access to a Company Profit and Net Value Share

Two issues raised by *Doing Business* directly relate to the expectations of minority investors in sharing the fruits of the company operations and growth. The first issue *Doing Business* explores in this regard is whether a mandate exists to share a portion of the company profits in the form of dividends. Such a policy would help ensure that a controlling shareholder is not diverting funds to salaries or other projects that might disproportionately favor him or her. It also could prevent a well-known method of forcing minority shareholders to capitulate and agree to leave the company.

Dividend freezing, despite company profits, can be particularly maleficent for minority investors in laws that force them to pay taxes on these profits, even though they are receiving no payments. Because a controlling investor can often point to seemingly reasonable pretexts for refusing to pay dividends, such distribution mandates might not be effective unless mandatory and proactive. At the same time, policy makers should be cautious of creating mandatory rules that compromise company reserves and, thereafter, negotiators should be relatively satisfied with the agreement, at least from a legal risk perspective. There should be policies that help minority investors maintain the arrangements they have negotiated or to comfortably adjust to new conditions that might arise.

Institutions Facilitating Minority Investor Protection

Without effective supervision and enforcement, the letter of law and regulations have little meaning. The availability of competent and responsive institutions to enforce rights in the law books is even more important for investors of privately held companies. Such investors cannot simply sell their shares in response to corporate wrongdoing. Further, because privately held companies tend to be less well known, these companies are generally less susceptible to bad publicity that minority investors might be able to generate if they have uncovered misdeeds in corporate governance. This urges institutions and other mechanisms, including government agencies, courts, and alternative dispute resolution mechanisms, to facilitate minority investor protection.

Government Agencies

An important factor in enforcing minority investor rights in publicly traded companies is the work of security regulators and, in many cases, stock exchange and self-regulatory organizations.

Courts

Most of the burden of enforcing the rights of minority investors in privately held companies falls on investors themselves. Their primary source for the vindication of their rights is the court system where the company they have invested in is incorporated.

Egypt Business Regulation: Benchmarking

We have to know the economic situation of Egypt before starting any new investment. Benchmarking is a tool we use to measure your current situation with regard to others. The strength of business environment is scored on the basis of economy performance in each of the 10 areas included in the Ease of Doing Business ranking. In the Ease of Doing Business ranking, Egypt scored 114 out of 190, with score being 60.1 as shown in Figure 7.1.

It takes multiple times longer than normal to begin a business in the economies positioned in the last 50 than it does in the top 20. Moving property in the 20 top economies requires under two weeks, contrasted with around a quarter of a year in the last 50. Getting a power association in a normal base-50 economy takes twice the time it takes in a normal top-20 economy. The expense of such an association is multiple times higher when communicated as a portion of pay per capita. Likewise, business contest goals endure about 2.1 years in economies positioned in the last 50 contrasted with 1.1 years in those positioned in the top 20. Outstanding contrasts among the more grounded and

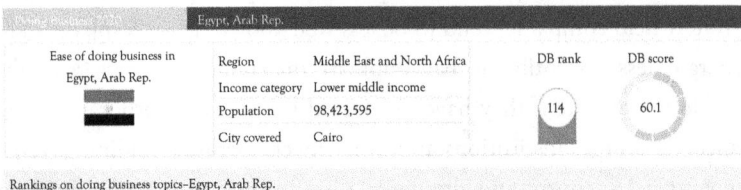

Figure 7.1 Egypt business regulation: benchmarking

more vulnerable performing economies are likewise clear in the nature of guidelines and data.

The Cost of Starting a Business Has Fallen Over Time in Developing Economics

Nowadays, there is a big opportunity of doing business for low-middle-income economies than last years. The steps and measurement of opening new business are discussed in the following pages.

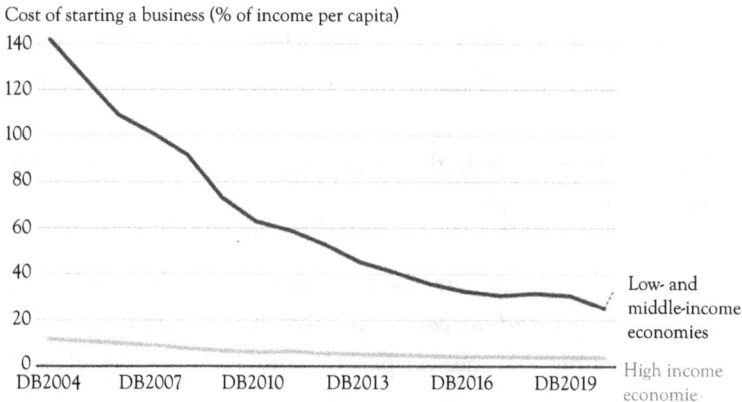

Cost of starting a business (% of income per capita)

Figure 7.2 *The cost of starting a business has fallen over time in developing economics*

Source: Doing Business–Embed this chart–Download Image

The Steps and Measurement of Opening a New Business

1. Starting a Business
In Egypt, to start a new limited liability business, it needs the efforts of five men and takes 12 days to obtain and finalize the paper work of registration for the new business with cost 20.3 percent income per capita.

Starting a Business in the Arab Republic of Egypt—Scores

Procedures: 73.6
Time: 87.9
Cost 89.9
Paid-in minimum capital 100

These are the 12 indicators to measure ease of Doing Business ranking of 190 economies of the world

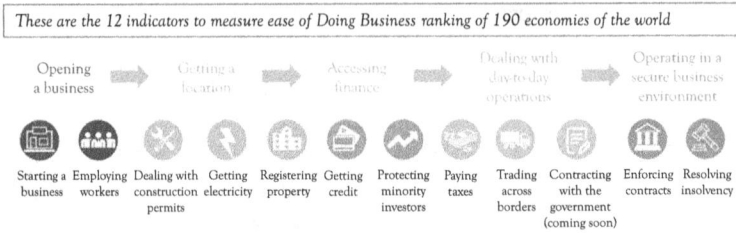

Figure 7.3 The steps and measurement of opening new business

Note: The employing workers and contracting with the government indicator sets are not included in the ease of doing business ranking.

Meanwhile, to start the same business with the same specifics but by women, it needs 6 women and 13 days to finalize the registration process with same cost.

The procedures of obtain the required registrations for a new limited liability business in Egypt:

1. *Submit documents, pay the fees, and receive the certificate of incorporation and tax card.* This takes three to four days, and the cost varies per each needed paper according to the capital of the business.

2. *Notarize company contracts.* This takes one day to be done, and it is free of charge.

3. *Open a company file and register employees with the national authority of social insurance.* This is the longest procedure to be obtained as it takes up to seven days, and it is also free of charge.

4. *Register for VAT* (**value-added taxes**). This procedure takes up to three days to be obtained from the Tax Authority, and it is free of charges.

5. *Buy and notarize company books.* This procedure takes place simultaneously with the registration for VAT procedure, and it might take one day to be finalized free of charge.

6. *Obtain a work permit from husband.* This procedure is for women only as they need to obtain a permission from the husband to leave the martial home and go out for work provided that they do not misuse this right, and their work does not conflict with their family interests.

2. Dealing with Construction Permits

This is the second step, which is building a warehouse, and it measures the procedures, time, and cost for obtaining the necessary licenses, permits, and submitting all required notifications.

In Egypt, building a warehouse requires 20 men and 173 days with the estimated value of EGP 2,199,243.60, and this costs about 1.3 percent of the warehouse value.

Dealing With Construction Permits in the Arab Republic of Egypt—Scores

Procedures: 40

Time: 57.6

Cost: 93.7

Building quality control index: 93.3

The procedures of dealing with constructions permits in Egypt:

1. **Apply for site validity certificate:** This procedure takes one calendar day at the Municipal Authority and costs EGP 200.
2. **Receive on-site inspection from the municipality:** An inspector from the Municipal Engineering Department inspects the construction site before obtaining the site validity certificate. This would take one day, and it is free of charge.
3. **Obtain site validity certificate from the municipality:** It takes up to 15 days to obtain the site validity for construction certificate, and it is also free of charge.
4. **Obtain a geotechnical study/soil test:** This step is simultaneously done with obtaining the validity certificate. It takes up to 9 days and costs EGP 4,500.
5. **Request and obtain building permit from the municipality:** This procedure takes 30 days and costs EGP 3,465 to be finalized.
6. **Hire an external engineer to supervise the construction site:** While the request to obtain building permits is being processed, the company needs to hire an independent engineer to supervise the constructions. This requires one day and costs EGY 2,000.

7. **Obtain approval of the execution supervision certificate from the Syndicate of Licensed Engineers:** This takes one day and costs EGP 416.

8. **Inform the municipality before beginning construction:** This procedure takes one day, and it is free of charge.

9. **Receive setback inspection from the municipality (I, II, III):** Each procedure requires one day for the inspection by the municipality, and it is free of charge.

10. **Obtain approval of construction conformity certificate from the Syndicate of Licensed Engineers:** This certificate must be signed by the supervising engineer and approved by the Syndicate of Engineers. It takes one day and costs EGP 300.

11. **Request and receive on-site inspection from the Civil Defense and Firefighting Authority:** This step takes 15 days and with no charge.

12. **Submit the construction conformity certificate and receive final inspection from the Municipality:** This step also takes 15 days with no cost.

13. **Register the building with the Real Estate Registry.**

3. Getting Electricity

This step is required to obtain permanent electricity supply for the newly constructed warehouse. In Egypt, to obtain the permanent electricity from South Cairo Electricity Distribution Company (SCEDC), this requires five men, 53 days, and 180.2 percent income per capita.

Getting Electricity in the Arab Republic of Egypt—Scores

Procedures: 66.7
Time: 84.8
Cost: 97.8
Reliability of supply and transparency of tariff index: 62.5

4. Registering Property

This step is the standardized case for an entrepreneur to purchase and register a land and a building. It measures the quality of the land from five aspects: reliability of infrastructure, transparency of information, geographic coverage, land dispute resolution, and equal access to property rights.

In Egypt, this procedure requires nine men, 76 days with cost 1.1 percent of the property value, and the quality of the land administration index, which is determined by scale from 0 to 30. The quality of land in Egypt is 9 on the quality scale.

Registering Property in the Arab Republic of Egypt—Scores

Procedures: 33.3
Time: 64.1
Cost: 92.7
Quality of the land administration index: 30

5. Getting Credit

This step relates to getting funds, assessing the lending facilities, and bankruptcy laws.

In Egypt, the strength of the legal right index, which provides production of secure creditor rights is 5, depth of credit information index is 8, while the percentage of adult population in the largest credit bureau is 31.5, and credit registry is 9.5.

Getting Credit in the Arab Republic of Egypt—Scores

Getting credit: 65

6. Protecting Minority Investors

This step is the protection assessment for the shareholders from the personal misuse of the assets by the managing directors.

**Protecting Minority Investors in the Arab
Republic of Egypt—Scores**

Protecting minority investors: 64.0

7. Paying Taxes

This step pertains to monitoring and listing the taxes and mandatory contribution that is forced by law within the fiscal year, and assigning on whom these tax reports, compliance, and payment burden falls. In Egypt, the number of payments/year including consumption taxes is 27; the time required to collecting information, preparing separate taxes, completing tax return, arranging payment is 370 hour per year; the percentage of profit or corporate income tax, the social contribution labor taxes paid by the employer, and the financial transaction taxes are 44.4.

Paying Taxes in the Arab Republic of Egypt—Scores

Payments: 60.0

Time: 50.4

Total tax and contribution rate: 73.9

Postfiling index: 36.6

8. Trading Across Borders

This step discusses and measures the cost and time of exporting the company comparative advantage product and importing the needed parts to carry over the business.

In Egypt, time to export, border compliance per hour is 48, while the cost to export, border compliance is USD 258.

Time to export, documentary compliance per hour is 88 (preparing and submitting documents during transport, clearance and the documents required by the destination economy, all documents required by law and in practice), while the cost to export, documentary compliance is USD 100.

Time to import, border compliance per hour is 240 (handling and inspections that take place at the economy port or border), while the cost to import, border compliance per year is USD 554.

Time to import, documentary compliance per hour is 265 (loading or unloading of the shipment at the warehouse or port/border), while the cost to export, documentary compliance is USD 1000.

Trading across Borders in the Arab Republic of Egypt—Scores

Time to export: border compliance: 70.4

Cost to export: border compliance: 75.5

Time to export: documentary compliance: 48.5

Cost to export: documentary compliance: 75.0

Time to import: border compliance: 14.3

Cost to import: border compliance: 53.9

Time to import: documentary compliance: 0.0

Cost to import: documentary compliance: 0.0

9. Enforcing Contracts

This indicator estimates the time and cost that may result in resolving any commercial dispute in front of a local first—instance court and also evaluating the quality for judicial process index among countries and the efficiency of the court system.

In Egypt, time (days) for filing and serving cases, trill seeking and obtaining judgment, and for enforcing judgment is 1,010 days, while the percentage cost of claiming value through courts, which includes court cost average, attorney fees, and enforcement costs, is 26.2, and for quality of judicial processes, court structure and proceedings, and case management is 4.0.

Enforcing Contracts in the Arab Republic of Egypt—Scores

Time 27.0

Cost: 70.6

Quality of judicial processes index: 22.2

10. Resolving Insolvency

This step measures the time and cost of resolving insolvency if it occurred among countries.

In Egypt, the time required to recover debt (years), measured by calendar and extensions are also included, is 2.5, while the percentage cost of recovered debt (court fees, law fees, insolvency administrators) is 22.0, of outcome (whether business continues operating as a going concern or business assets are sold piecemeal) is 0, and of insolvency framework index, of commencement, of proceedings index, and of reorganization proceedings index is 9.5.

Resolving Insolvency in the Arab Republic of Egypt—Scores

Recovery rate: 25.1

Strength of insolvency framework index: 59.4

Conclusion

As per this study, Egypt has a comparative advantage in starting a new business in some rankings. Egypt got the highest scores in facilitating the establishment of a new business with a score 87.5 percent higher than the other economic capitals.

CHAPTER 8

The Entrepreneurial Mindset in the SME Sector

Introduction

Business success in the new economy is not merely a function of relevant skills but also requires people who have entrepreneurial mindsets. The key objective of this chapter is to determine the entrepreneurial mindset of Small and medium enterprises (SMEs) in general. SMEs are defined as separate and distinct commercial entities in some countries, in addition to their branches or subsidiaries. McGrath and MacMillan (2000) assert that an entrepreneurial mindset, which consists of elements such as goal orientation, hunting profitable opportunities, extreme discipline, and embracing a strong personal inner drive, is of utmost importance for any business to make ends meet. Kiyosaki and Letcher (2003) point out that not all business owners have the required "entrepreneurial mindset" to become successful, which is an essential concept to business success. There is no rule to follow to be an entrepreneur, so how is it possible to be one? This is not an easy question to answer because there is no role model for entrepreneurs, but in this chapter, we attempt to discuss how an entrepreneur thinks. We focus on how entrepreneurs who start SMEs think.

There are some factors that most successful entrepreneurs pay attention to. Here, we focus on the six most important aspects that successful entrepreneurs do. They always think big seeing the whole picture. They work on their business, not in it. They are risk takers, but they also know how to minimize or mitigate those risks. Regarding growth, they prefer small sustainable jumps rather than big unstudied growth. They know how to play in the new markets. Finally, they prefer to build a system-dependent company not people-dependent company.

The Concept: Entrepreneurial Mindset

An entrepreneurial mindset refers to the way of thinking about business and its opportunities that capture the benefits of uncertainty. Scheepers (2009) believes that "an 'entrepreneurial mindset' needs an innovative, willing and energetic pursuit towards a specified opportunity, by means of rapid sensing, acting and mobilized responses, in order to achieve a maximum gain." Establishing an entrepreneurial mindset is important for sustaining the competitiveness of economic organizations and the socioeconomic lifestyle of the population through value and job creation (Dhliwayo and Vuuren 2007).

The Entrepreneurial Mind

Allen and Economy (2008) note that all entrepreneurs, habitual and accidental, have something like an "entrepreneurial mind," as they all perform tasks that include, but not are not limited to, the following:

1. Spotting fundamental changes to create opportunities
2. Creating niches in markets they can dominate
3. Putting customers at the center of everything they do
4. Implementing nonhierarchical teams
5. Forming strategic partnerships with other businesses

According to Nieman (2006), the failure of SMEs to either create job opportunities or grow is because of the perceived "mindset" of its owners. This is defined as one of the major causes of SMEs failure rates. Eno-Obong (2006) points out that entrepreneur with an entrepreneurial mindset can see the needs, problems, and challenges as opportunities. They develop innovative ways to deal with challenges and exploit and combine opportunities. McGrath and MacMillan (2000) argue that having an entrepreneurial mindset is the main reason for an individual to successfully move forward in an entrepreneurial process. Dhliwayo and Vuuren (2007) assert that an entrepreneurial mindset is significant for the success of SMEs, and without it, a business fails. According to Lotito, et al. (1997), this particular argument opens individuals/SMEs to modern styles of consciousness and helps them secure their place in business world.

Think Big

According to Johnson (2009), the first belief that the entrepreneur should have is "Think Big." Thinking big means you need to have a broad vision because lack of this is one of the main reasons for SMEs' failure. If you do not have a strategy, you will end up with either not surviving beyond the start or not getting the full potential of your business. A good example to discuss here is when an entrepreneur has a great idea, but he/she does not have a strategy to do it correctly. One of the biggest mistakes is to start even without a strategy to compete. Successful entrepreneurs always have a strategy from the beginning before paying one pound to pursue their ideas. There is no best strategy to use, but a start cannot be made without a strategy. In addition, successful entrepreneurs understand the tradeoff between the price and quality. Hence, they always focus on one factor as a competitive advantage. To act like an entrepreneur, one must get a strategy to work on before starting a small or medium business. As an entrepreneur, you must have a different point of view that is not limited by your environment. If you are an engineer, you should be able to see the world from your client point of view. If you are a doctor, you should be able to see the world from your patient point of view. However, this is not enough. You should go beyond this, and this is what is called "thinking out of the box." Thinking out of the box is not just when you get an innovative idea. It means that there are no limits to your ideas. Real entrepreneurs can invest in many different fields that are so far from their specialization. This happens because they are not limited with the environment. They always smell business opportunities. This is something gained by practice.

Work on Your Business, Not in Your Business

According to Johnson (2009), another belief that entrepreneurs should have is working on their business. Not doing this is one of the most common mistakes that real entrepreneurs understand very well and know how to avoid. As mentioned in the first role of thinking big, one of the targets you must set from Day one is building an operational system that is independent of you. Think if you would die tomorrow, would your business be able to continue or it would die with you? It is normal during the introduction and part of growth phases that you as an entrepreneur would wear multiple hats, but you must work on getting rid of that very quickly. Your role as an entrepreneur is not the execution. Your role is planning and building the operational system. Think about the day when you might decide to sell your running profitable business. Do you think that an investor would buy a one-man-show company? From now, you should understand that your time is much more valuable to spend on execution. This may occur for a limited time to give the first push to your company, but you should set a target to build a self-running business that is able to operate and grow without need for you.

Entrepreneur Is a Calculated Risk Taker

According to Scarborugh (2016), "An entrepreneur is one who creates a new business in the face of risk and uncertainty for the purpose of achieving profit and growth by identifying significant opportunities and assembling the necessary resources to capitalize on them." In addition, the economic prospective or classical definition of an entrepreneur is simply the risk taker. Does this mean, though, that the entrepreneur is a gambler? Of course, this is not what is meant by risk taker. Entrepreneurs take what is called a calculated risk, with risk being "the possibility of loss." Does this mean that someone who builds a business with a loss probability of 1 percent is an entrepreneur? Of course not. The difference is that an entrepreneur can go to more risky investments but with a good market study, hiring the appropriate staff, and managing the financial part of the project. This would decrease the risk of doing this business, and it is either a small or medium business.

Entrepreneurs Make Incremental Advances

According to Linkov, Bridges, Creutzig, Decker, Fox-Lent, Kröger, and Thiel-Clemen (2014), one of the lessons that entrepreneurs have been learned from the dot-com crash is that you cannot get very big jumps in a very short time. You have to get incremental steps, but those steps must be small and sustainable. This is how the growth happens in most successful businesses. If you were an earlier user of Facebook, for example, in

2004 or 2005, you can compare how it looks like now with how it was 15 years ago. Entrepreneurs building their start-up business must know this rule. You should not wait for the perfect model. The better option is to enhance as much as you can, then start the business with sustainable and constant growth rate. One of the known reasons for the failure of start-up companies is the unstudied growth. That would lead to many problems such as running out of cash or breaking the operational process that is not designed to handle this very high unexpected rate of orders.

Blue Ocean Is Always More Profitable

According to Linkov, Bridges, Creutzig, Decker, Fox-Lent, Kröger, and Thiel-Clemen (2014), one of the lessons in the start-up world is the rule that says "A competitive market destroys profits." This would lead us to another important question, which is how successful entrepreneurs think of marketing. To better describe what the blue ocean is, it is better to take it from the *Blue Ocean Strategy*, which is one of the best-selling business books. According to Kim (2005), "Blue ocean strategy challenges companies to break out of the red ocean of bloody competition by creating uncontested market space that makes the competition irrelevant." Finally, it is your decision to work as an evolutionary or revolutionary product, but most successful entrepreneurs prefer the revolutionary, which is the blue ocean strategy.

System Is More Important Than People

According to Johnson (2009), the next belief that an entrepreneur should embrace is to "[b]uild a company that is System-Dependent not People-Dependent." This is necessary to avoid one of the most common mistakes known for experienced entrepreneurs. Successful entrepreneurs understand very well that system building is more important than getting the best talents in the market. Think about McDonalds. Surely, it is not the best burger you could eat. However, it is one of the best restaurants that have a consistent and sustainable process. Suppose you are trying to open a restaurant like McDonalds, you should pay more attention to the process than the skills of the chiefs. If you visited 10 restaurants of McDonalds in the same country, you would certainly notice that the taste is the same exactly. However, the staff is different people who may have not ever met. This is the power of building an easy to use system. Of course, you still may need some highly skilled employees, but that must not be the default case. This is a common mistake in many SMEs, especially when the entrepreneur has a technical background like being a programmer for example. You may find him occupied all the time with writing and modifying some codes. However, he must be busy with building a system for programmers to work on. That is also one of the very known concepts in management, which is that a "manager must not be involved in the execution." Hence, an entrepreneur must not be trapped in process implementation. Rather, what must be focused on is process creation that would guarantee business continuity regardless of who would be involved in implementation. In addition, the job description and responsibilities for each member in the company must be clearly set.

Self-Theories and the Characteristics of the Entrepreneurial Mindset

Dweck (2006) developed two self-theories of intelligence by providing insight into the psychological (motivational) processes essential for achievement. She stated that individuals hold either an entity theory of intelligence, known as a fixed mindset, or an incremental theory of intelligence, known as a growth mindset. A core tenet for individuals with a fixed mindset is that intelligence, talents, abilities, and attributes are permanent and unchangeable. According to Dweck (2006), they further infer that one's ability come from talents rather than from their slow development of skills through learning, and as such, they give up or go into a decline in the face of setbacks. According to Johnson (2009), individuals with a fixed mindset, who have low confidence, tend to adopt low performance goals, which in turn causes them to respond in a helpless characteristic manner/pattern of typical behaviors, thoughts, and feelings when faced with challenges. Individuals with a growth mindset, on the other hand, believe that ability and success are based on learning, and that intelligence can be enhanced and change with effort. They also believe in trying other approaches, seeking help when faced with difficulties, and tending to adopt learning goals. Individuals with high or a low confidence respond with a typical response pattern of thoughts, behaviors, and feelings in any situation they face by focusing on learning new ideas (Johnson 2009). The reason of this is that most successful business leaders have a growth mindset.

The Impact of Training, Work Experience, and Education on the Entrepreneurial Mindset

A positive relationship has been established between education and business creation. The firm needed to educate and give training to maximize the returns. In this view, Timmons and Spinelli (2004) asserted that entrepreneurship education is very important as it can be taught, and it will contribute to job creation and create a great impact on poverty alleviation. Experience is an important factor in entrepreneurial success. Most literature studies have confirmed a positive relationship between the entrepreneur's experience, a firm's growth and survival of the businesses.

The Impact of Creativity and Motivation on Entrepreneurial Mindset and Business Success

According to Dhliwayo and Vuuren (2007), entrepreneurial mindset is about creativity, innovation, and catching opportunities that lead to the success of the organizational and wealth creation, and this type of mindset enables individual to make realistic decisions when they face uncertainties. Creativity is a means to unlock the entrepreneurial potential of individuals, entrepreneurs, and organizations, as new ideas is the key of promoting an entrepreneurial culture. Creativity is essential for the success of the organization. Encouraging creativity is a strategic decision that firms should take into consideration.

According to Dunnette and Hough (1990), motivation, on the other hand, reflects a complete psychological force that determines the person's behavior in the organization, the effort of the person, and a person's extent of persistence of the person to face of setbacks. Motivation helps entrepreneurs to acquire skills, knowledge, and abilities and thus provide the impetus and energy needed for implementing the action. Motivation can possibly separate individuals who positively evaluate opportunities from those who do not.

Entrepreneurial Characteristics and Their Impact on the Long-Term Survival of SMEs

What defines successful and potential entrepreneurs from different individual are those characteristics that are distinctive to them. O'Connor and Fiol (2002) defined entrepreneurial characteristics as a typical feature or quality that someone or somebody has such as being innovative, creative, and open to change, have the ability to identify opportunities and achieve stated goals, which can build something of recognized values around perceived opportunities. Neneh (2011) identified creativity, self-reliance, and ability to adapt; tolerance of ambiguity and uncertainty; opportunity obsession; commitment and determination to be the necessary entrepreneurial characteristics required for the long-term survival of SMEs. This study, thus, adopts these characteristics established by Neneh (2011) as the necessary characteristics for the long-term survival of SMEs.

The Entrepreneurial Mindset in Egypt

Egypt has witnessed a dynamic entrepreneurial movement that had started to take place among youth and young professionals in Egypt and the region. Egyptian society's perception of entrepreneurship is particularly high and continues to grow. More than 73 percent of Egyptians think entrepreneurship is a good career choice. While more than 30 percent of Egyptians shy away from starting a new business due to fear of failure, 46 percent of Egypt's adult population is actually able to recognize good market opportunities for new businesses, perhaps suggesting that more people have the capability and knowledge to be entrepreneurs.

Entrepreneurship and Job Creation

Entrepreneurship and job creation have recently become buzzwords used by the country private sector and civil society leaders as a way to develop and stabilize Egypt. Numerous scholarly pieces and technical reports have been produced on the state of entrepreneurship in Egypt and the Arab world, on the necessity of entrepreneurship for fostering more inclusive economic growth, and on the region's glaring unemployment rate. The focus on entrepreneurship is not surprising, given the role that it can play in tackling unemployment. A well-directed entrepreneurship ecosystem can offer a sustainable solution to the country's most pressing socioeconomic challenges—unemployment and inequity—while at the same time sparking a culture of innovation. Literature on what is needed to support an increase in sustainable and scalable start-up enterprises references several weaknesses in Egypt's entrepreneurship ecosystem. These weaknesses range from issues with existing legal frameworks to the availability and accessibility of financing options to problems with the educational system.

Legal Frameworks

A cumbersome and complicated registration system had been a major barrier to entering the market and prevented already existing informal enterprises from formalizing. While economic reforms introduced in 2004 dealt with issues of registration, contract enforcement and taxation remain barriers to entrepreneurial growth. Doing business in Egypt also continues to be an easier endeavor for those who are well connected, decreasing the chances of the marginalized and those with minimal social capital from entering formal markets and exiting poverty. Yet even those who are well connected and affluent struggle to take their businesses to scale, as can be seen from the overall size of the Egyptian private sector, which remains far from its potential.

Access to Capital

Access to capital has been another major barrier for entrepreneurs from different walks of life, especially youth. Major banks and financial institutions are biased in favor of larger and less risky constituencies of the market, with the accompanying strong belief that start-ups and existing SMEs are not bankable. The introduction of the Social Fund for Development (SFD) in 1991 was an important step toward making small loans available to young people, but it has failed to create a booming SME sector. A dearth of financial literacy has prevented youth from utilizing opportunities like the SFD, given their lack of awareness and understanding of loaning schemes and the negligible risk associated with them. Aside from the SFD, available financing options are mainly limited to a select segment of the population—those who are well educated and English literate.

In addition, up until recently, alternative nonbanking financing mechanisms such as venture capital, private equity, and crowdfunding have been absent from the Egyptian market. It has only been lately that such financing options have emerged; these include entities such as Sawari Ventures. Vodafone Ventures, Ideavelopers, the Cairo Angel Investors. Delta Shield, Ahead of the Curve, and Shekra. Most of these alternative financing options are primarily focused on tech-based entrepreneurs. Further, the Egyptian American Enterprise Fund (EAEF), though announced in President Obama's 2011 Cairo speech, was not officially launched until March 2013. The EAEF commenced with $60 million from the U.S. government, with hopes of reaching $300 million in three years. To date, the EAEF has yet to disperse loans or equity investments, and it remains unclear how the fund will strategically go about supporting start-ups and SMEs. Moreover, the amount of money pledged by the United States for this fund is minute compared to the needs required, and in the case of Egypt, it is miniscule in contrast to the amount of U.S. dollars invested in military aid. Nonetheless, if the fund takes off, it can play an important role in the ecosystem alongside the already existing local players.

Education

A third principal barrier to fostering entrepreneurship in Egypt has been the country's public educational system, namely the fact that it does not teach an entrepreneurial mindset, including risk-taking and innovative thinking. Youth are not equipped with basic entrepreneurial skills such as business development, which is required for business expansion. Fortunately, the new equity financing options aforementioned were introduced with acceleration and incubation packages that provide start-up entrepreneurs with the needed business development and mentorship support services. Such an introduction to the ecosystem has significantly changed the landscape, as it leads entrepreneurs through the hardships of starting a business in Egypt. Also, some entrepreneurship education programs have been introduced to private universities such as the American University in Cairo (AUC) and the British University in Egypt (BUE). Injaz Egypt has launched a unique program with the aim of raising awareness of entrepreneurship and entrepreneurial skills among young adults. More recently, Silatech and Microsoft Egypt have partnered to make basic entrepreneurial resources, such as business plan writing resources, available online through an English and Arabic portal. Informal awareness and educational opportunities offered through seminars and networking events on the topic are also available in urban centers like Cairo and Alexandria. Yet with the exception of Injaz and Microsoft/Silatech's efforts, entrepreneurship education and awareness efforts are primarily accessible to well-educated and English-literate individuals.

After the 25th of January revolution, the youth was going to have ambitious ideas regarding the life in Egypt, including justice, living conditions, and job opportunities; however, all these expectations were not met, and people were frustrated, specially after the slowdown in economic growth, which led to high unemployment rates and job losses. These issues affected the quality of available job opportunities, and people in Egypt were divided. Some were seeking jobs even if these jobs were not enough for their qualifications. Others, though, thought that they should think out of the box and try to make some changes as independence and leaving positive impact on their society. These factors contributed to increasing interest in entrepreneurship in Egypt. Entrepreneurship has a magnificent effect on country economy. It does not only provide job opportunities but also impacts the whole economy by fostering competition, productivity, innovation, and provides an opportunity to include more segments of society. SMEs in Egypt already contribute to the economy as they play a vital role in the national economy, which countries depend on as a major means of development. They have become one of the strongest social and economic growth tools and the most important strategic elements in the process of development and growth.

Based on global competitiveness reports, I made a simple comparison between the years 2018 and 2019 about the factors affected, and following are the conclusions reached.

Egypt was raised one level from ranking 94 out of 141 in 2018 to 93 in 2019, even though it is still in the same ranking compared to the Middle East and north African countries. The index includes the following 12

Egypt

93rd / 141

Global Competitiveness Index 4.0 2019 edition

Rank in 2018 edition: 94th /140

Performance Overview 2019   Key ◆ Previous edition   ▲ Lower-middle-income group average   ☐ Middle East and North Africa average

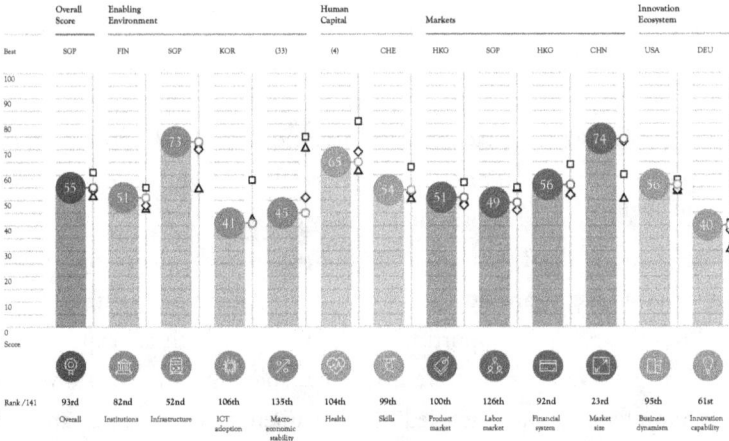

Selected contextual indicators			
Population millions	97.0	GDP (PPP) % world GDP	0.96
GDP per capita US$	2,573.3	5-year average FDI inward flow % GDP	2.6
10-year average annual GDP growth %	3.3		

Social and environmental performance

Figure 8.1 Factors affected in the performance 2019

main pillars, which are divided into subindicators: Institution, infrastructure, adoption of information and communication technology, macroeconomics, health, skills, product market, labor market, financial system, market size, business dynamics, and innovation capability.

In, 2018, Infrastructure ranked 56, Market Size 24, Macroeconomic Stability 135, and Labor Market 130. In 2019, Egypt made good achievement at the best pillars, which are Infrastructure (ranking 52) and Market Size (ranking 23), while in the two pillars of Macroeconomic Stability and Labor Market, the ranks were (135)—same as in the 2018 index— and (126), respectively.

Although there was great improvement in the Institution pillar as it ranked 82 in 2019 and 102 in 2018, we are still in a late ranking in some of the subindicators as the Terrorism Incidence got rank 136 (compared to 135 in 2018) and Freedom of the Press ranked 132 (same as 2018), while Government Responsiveness to change was at its best as it ranked 23 out of 141.

Apart from the Institution pillars and the factors that could affect the entrepreneur eco-system in Egypt, we should focus on some subindicators in that pillar such as Public Sector Performance, Transparency, Corporate Governance, and Future Orientation of Government as these subindicators will help in improving business start-up companies and finally will affect the whole system of entrepreneurship. For the Infrastructure pillars, Egypt made a good progress from 2018 (was ranked 56) as it ranked 52 in 2019, and the best subindicator under this pillar was Liner Shipping Connectivity (ranking 18 in 2019 compared to 26 in 2018). We can see that we achieved great performance in connecting the shipping and marine systems with the world, as we have many ports that can carry great numbers of vessels. This can be a great indicator for entrepreneurship, especially after all the recent projects supported by the government.

Followed by Liner Shipping is Quality of Road Infrastructure, which also made great improvement by moving from 45 in 2018 to 28 in 2019.

The lowest subindicator in that pillar is the Electricity Supply Quality, which ranked 77. Accordingly, we should make some efforts to improve the system of electricity supply.

For the Information Communications Technology (ICT) Adoption, Egypt stepped back six levels from 2018 to rank 106 in the 2019 report. All the subindicators of that pillar ranked very low in that report, thus indicating that there is a need for implementing the entrepreneur system and trying to apply it in Egypt to improve the system of broadband Internet subscription.

In Macroeconomic Stability, Egypt did not make progress from 2018 as it ranked the same (135). In Health, we stepped back five places from 99 in 2018 to 104 in 2019. As for the Skills pillar, Egypt made no progress also from 2018 as it ranked 99. This pillar should be considered especially if we are talking about entrepreneurship.

Egypt scored 11 levels up in the Product Market pillar ranking 100 globally, and the best subindicator was represented in the Services Competition Index (33 globally), while the worst subindicator was represented in the Trade Tariffs, where Egypt ranked 136, followed by the Complexity of Tariff at the 86th position globally.

Egypt scored also four positions in the Labor Market pillar ranking 126 globally out of 130 in 2018. The best subindicator was Flexibility of Wage Determination, which came in the 14th ranking globally, while the worst subindicators were Ratio of Wage and Salaried Female Workers to Male Workers in the 131st global ranking.

With regard to the Financial System, Egypt moved seven points ahead from 99 in 2018 to 92 in 2019. The Soundness of Banks indicator was the best of this pillar as it ranked 23 followed by Financing of SMEs, which ranked 41. The worst indicator in this pillar was the Credit Gap Index, which ranked 124 on the global scale.

As for the Market Size pillar, which was the best ranked pillar on the global scale, it moved one point ahead in 2019 to become 23. Egypt achieved two points progress in its rank regarding Business Dynamism to become 95 on the global scale. Growth of Innovative Companies came as the best subindicator (ranking 29), while the worst indicators was the Index of the Cost of Starting a Business, which ranked 124 globally.

Concerning Innovation Capability, Egypt improved its situation, ranking 61 in 2019 compared to 64 in 2018. Diversity of Workforce was the best indicator ranking the 12th globally, while the worst indicators were Trademark Application followed by Patent Applications ranking 101st and 92nd, respectively.

Entrepreneurship varies across countries and depends not only on economic growth but also on other factors according to the global competitiveness report. To make entrepreneurial improvement, which could be a key factor in reaching the next stage of development, we should work on the Skills pillar by improving critical thinking in teaching, the quality of vocational training, and the skills of graduates as this could help boost the entrepreneurship system. This added value requires highly skilled workforce capable of performing complex tasks and who can adapt quickly to the changing needs of consumers. Therefore, the role of education and training is crucial for countries seeking development. Moreover, increasing the productivity and competitiveness of a country requires a workforce as healthy as possible. Poor health will result in a low yield of work and a significant cost to business. Therefore, investment in health is vital for sustainable economy. Macroeconomic stability is also important for business and, therefore, for the overall competitiveness of a country. It is true that macroeconomic stability should be cumulative with a number of other determinants in order to enhance competitiveness. Without technology and networking, we cannot make any step forward in any field, especially entrepreneurship, as it is strongly connected to them. The institutional environment of a country depends on the efficiency and behavior of involved stakeholders, both public and private. The legal and administrative framework in which individuals, firms, and governments interact determines the quality of public institutions of a country, and it has a strong influence on competitiveness and growth. It influences investment decisions, including entrepreneurship, and it plays a key role in the ways in which societies distribute benefits and bear the costs of development strategies and policies.

Finally, all these factors contribute to build a country with entrepreneurial vision, and the main factor and indicator to measure this is SMEs. In Egypt, SMEs play a vital role in the national economy, which countries depend on as a major focus of development. They have become one of the strongest social and economic growth tools and the most important strategic element in development and growth. Entrepreneurship is a very important activity for the competitiveness and growth of a country and a significant source of social mobility. New ventures have become an important aspect of country economic development, especially in terms of their contributions to new job creation.

There is a strong relationship between SMEs and entrepreneur ventures. They are interrelated as entrepreneurial ventures are not just concerned with making money. They want to make more. They are the ones that dare to shake up a market by introducing an innovative product or feature or become the most recognized brand from the quality of service or production. Entrepreneurial ventures are typically founded with a great idea or concept behind them, while small businesses are not always concerned with growing or becoming more profitable. They just care about the work they do day to day. Their goal is to ensure longevity and continual development.

Conclusion

In sum, entrepreneurship is a very important variable with enormous importance for country growth, especially in Egypt. Its importance increases as countries grow in terms of competitiveness and economic growth and move on to new stages of development that require a systematic and clear structure for support and promotion. We need to look for more opportunities to create a market open for youth to innovate and make creative ideas, which can result in a useful outcome to our economy. We should all make some effort to help boost country growth by supporting innovators and creative people. Entrepreneurs should adopt the ideal entrepreneurial mindset (passionately pursuing new opportunities with enormous discipline, pursuing only the very best opportunities, focusing on execution, and engaging everyone's energy in their domain) (McGrath and MacMillan 2000). Establishing an entrepreneurial mindset is important for sustaining business continuity.

CHAPTER 9

Global Entrepreneurship Monitor (GEM)

Introduction

The Global Entrepreneurship Research Association (GERA), the research consortium that carries out the Global Entrepreneurship Monitor (GEM) research program on an annual basis, has contributed to a deeper understanding of national differences in entrepreneurial attitudes, activity, and aspirations, and the characteristics of the environmental conditions that may either encourage or deter entrepreneurship. Since 1999, when the first GEM study appeared, information has been presented for more than 100 economies worldwide. As such, the GEM research program helps governments, businesses, and educators around the world to design policies and programs aimed at stimulating entrepreneurship. The GEM research project focuses on three main objectives: to measure the scale and scope of entrepreneurial activity and analyze how this differs across countries; to uncover factors determining national levels of entrepreneurial activity; to identify policies that may lead to appropriate levels of entrepreneurial activity.

GEM started in 1997 as a partnership between the London Business School and Babson College. In 1999, 10 national teams conducted the first GEM global study. The GEM research program has always been based on a harmonized assessment of the level of national entrepreneurial activity for all participating countries, using data from surveys of representative samples of the adult population in each participating economy. The National Expert Survey (NES) provides a wealth of data.

GEM website is a worldwide study on entrepreneurship that was started in 1997 by two academics. Its first published report came out in 1999 covering just 10 countries, but the number of countries has grown substantially ever since to cover more than 100 countries across all levels

of economic development and regions. GEM constitutes the single largest program to systematically research the prevalence, determinants, and
consequences of entrepreneurial activity on an international level. Since
its inception, over one million telephone interviews have been conducted
in 85 different countries to gather primary data on entrepreneurial activity, assuming that an interview lasted two minutes on average. The GEM
research project was designed as a long-term multinational endeavor with
the purpose of providing a database to study the complex relationship
between entrepreneurship and economic growth and facilitating evi-
dence-based policies that enhance entrepreneurship.

GEM collects internationally comparable data on entrepreneurial
activity in more than 50 countries in the world. It is a unique database
because there is no other source for comparable data on entrepreneurship from so many different countries. Unlike existing national statistics, GEM captures all kinds of entrepreneurial activities. It also captures
start-up efforts at a very early stage. GEM was started as and still sees itself
as a policy research project aimed at measuring and describing entrepreneurial activity, rather than testing any particular theoretical concepts.
As such, it has been enormously successful. The project has had a major
impact on policy making and public opinion. In particular, we address
the following research questions:

- How do researchers currently use GEM data in academic
  research in terms of the level of analysis, variables, methods,
  measurement scheme, and analytical procedures?
- What are best practices and problematic fields of application?
- How can future studies use the GEM database to its full potential?

The Global Entrepreneurship Monitor
as a Research Program

The GEM research program was initiated in 1997 to address the problem
that national statistics on newly established firms were not internationally comparable. There were no harmonized cross-national data available,
causing severe gaps in empirical entrepreneurship research. The aims of
GEM are to measure differences in the level of entrepreneurial activity

among countries, to uncover factors determining national levels of entrepreneurial activity, and to identify policies that may enhance the national level of entrepreneurial activity.

A pilot data collection project was carried out in 1998 with five participating countries. In the following years, this number increased continuously, and in 2010, 59 countries participated. To secure international comparability, GEM collects primary empirical data in a standardized way.

There are three main data sources:

- The Adult Population Survey (APS) provides standardized data on entrepreneurial activities and attitudes within each country.
- The NES investigates the national framework conditions for entrepreneurship by means of standardized questionnaires.
- Qualitative face-to-face interviews (national expert interviews) are being conducted to get a deeper understanding of the strengths, weaknesses, and major issues regarding entrepreneurship in the respective country.

There are limits to the length of the questionnaire, and it is mostly single items. As a global research project, the aim is to collect representative data in as many countries as possible. This can only be done by keeping the questionnaire relatively short and avoiding answer options that might lead to translation errors or cultural biases, which is a major reason for using binary (yes/no) responses. Including lengthy multi-item scales would also reduce the completion rate and might lead to a nonresponse bias.

Over time, a number of new questions were added to the questionnaire, and others were changed or dropped. However, the main structure of the APS questionnaire has remained unchanged since the year 1999. Reynolds, Bosma, Autio, Hunt, De Bono, Servais, Lopez-Garcia, and Chin (2005) describe the interview structure of the GEM 2003 APS that, to a large extent, is still valid today. In 2006, a new section on former self-employment was introduced. At present, the questionnaire consists of five sections.

Section 1 includes questions for all respondents. Screening items concerning entrepreneurial activity are included in this section, that is, whether people are currently trying to start a new business, are owner-managers of a company, expect to start a business, are active as an informal investors, or have shut down or quit a business they owned and managed. These screening questions are of great importance because they determine who is considered a nascent entrepreneur, business owner-manager, informal investor, or former business owner-manager.

Sections 2, 3, 4, and 5 are on nascent entrepreneurial activity, existing businesses, informal investment activity, and previous entrepreneurial activity, respectively.

Methodology and Framework

We applied a structured literature search and compiled an overall inventory of 109 articles. We only selected empirical studies that use data from the GEM APS. The focus is on contributions written in English and published in academic journals from the beginning of the GEM program in 1999 until the end of 2010. We only included articles from peer-reviewed journals, as they can be considered to convey the most scientifically validated knowledge with the highest impact in the field. GEM is an international project, and thus, articles are published in different parts of the world while SSCI rankings tend to have an Anglo-American bias (Andersen, Cobbold, and Lawrie 2001).

We excluded empirical studies that only used data from the expert survey as well as conceptual contributions concerning the methodology or the model underlying the GEM project. We also did not consider studies that merely referred to some key figures of the GEM project without conducting their own data analyses. Our search left us with a list of 109 articles that met our aforementioned selection criteria.

Results on the Use of GEM Data in Line With
Our Analyzing Framework

Data sources: This contribution only considers articles based on the GEM data.

1. Variables: Used dependent variables to increase our knowledge about relationships between different phenomena. Quantitative

research usually distinguishes between one (or more) dependent variable(s) and a set of independent variables with the assumption being that the independent variables influence or determine the dependent variable(s).

2. Level of analysis: More than two decades ago, Low and MacMillan observed that the success of the individual enterprise will be affected by factors that can only be observed at different levels of analysis.

3. Hypotheses.

4. Measurement schemes.

5. Statistical procedures: To capture the statistical procedures used in the studies.

Egypt Participated in GEM

Egypt participated in GEM cycles along with many other countries to monitor its entrepreneurial performance. The 2017/2018 report that will be summarized happens to be the sixth report covering Egypt. It is developed by a team of researchers from the American University in Cairo (AUC). GEM examines the factors that contribute to an entrepreneurial climate and the links between entrepreneurship and economic growth. Perspectives on entrepreneurship in Egypt are distributed as follows.

Societal Perception of Entrepreneurship

This perspective remains favorable as 75.9 percent of Egyptians perceive it as a good career choice (ranking seventh among GEM countries). About 43.5 percent of the nonentrepreneurs perceived an opportunity to start a new venture. This represents a drop from previous years, which could be a result of economic challenges such as the devaluation of the currency and reduction of subsidies, which have resulted in significant inflation.

Entrepreneurial Intention

This remains high with 55.5 percent of the Egyptian nonentrepreneurs surveyed, indicating interest in starting a new business within the next three years. Business discontinuation in Egypt has alarmingly increased over the past years from 2.7 percent in 2010 to 10.2 percent in 2017 with a consistent increasing pattern throughout the years in between the two mentioned ones. This consistency over an extended duration of time suggests that a large number and growing population of business owners and entrepreneurs discontinued their business. This could also be a result of the challenging economic environment and reduced overall opportunity. With regard to motivation for entrepreneurs to start their businesses, opportunity-driven entrepreneurship has been decreasing as 53.5 percent of the early-stage entrepreneurs reported that they were driven by market opportunity. However, 42.7 percent of early-stage entrepreneurs remain driven by necessity, and their number increased compared to the previous years.

Gender Distribution in Egypt

Almost one in every 3.5 entrepreneurs is a woman. In addition, women-led businesses have a lower probability of continuation compared to men-led businesses. The rate of women participation in Egypt is much lower than global averages.

Age Distribution

There is a noticeable increase in the percentage of youth who decide to start their own business. This growth in youth entrepreneurship maybe due to higher awareness and interest in having an independent career.

Sectorial Distribution

Most early-stage entrepreneurs are concentrated in three sectors: wholesale and retail distribution, manufacturing, and agricultural. These sectors are typically attractive for necessity entrepreneurs who happen to run informal micro/small enterprises.

It is also worth mentioning that job creation projections and growth orientation are divergent. On the one hand, 52.5 percent of Egyptian early-stage entrepreneurs do not expect to add any new jobs to their businesses within the first five years of their projects. This gives an indication of high self-employment businesses, which is typical in the case of necessity-driven informal micro enterprises. On the other hand, 23.7 percent of early-stage entrepreneurs expect to grow their business by six or more jobs within five years, reflecting high growth intention.

It can be concluded from all the aforementioned comparisons and statistics that despite the economic challenges in 2016, there seemed to be a positive trend in entrepreneurship in Egypt. More entrepreneurs are launching their start-ups, and positive societal perception of entrepreneurship is gaining ground. There is a strong recognition for market opportunities and a clear foundation for growing this sector.

Based on the concerned report, there were some recommendations made in order to support entrepreneurship in Egypt. Following are some key recommendations of those given by the experts:

- Include entrepreneurship in universities and school curricula as that is where the foundation of a person is formed.
- Expand incubators outside Cairo. Egypt is wide and full of potential, great minds, and opportunities. It is true that Cairo is a great environment to test new ideas and is a fertile soil for entrepreneurs, but there are a lot of places in Egypt that are thirsty for new business ideas.
- Work on developing an entrepreneurial and risk-taking culture among youth and overall society. A lot of business ideas do not require a big capital nor a lot of employees to kick start. They just require taking a risk on a brand new idea and being brave enough to launch it. Most of the new start-ups that made a huge impact such as Uber and Airbnb did not even require owning one car or a single apartment, yet they were and still are leading the whole world in the industry of transportation and house rentals. This is why, Egypt should spread the entrepreneurial culture and teach children that thinking out of the box is their only way to shine and make extraordinary profits and success.
- Adjust government policies in order to facilitate and enable better access to finance and other nonfinancial resources. It is already very hard and bureaucratic in Egypt when it comes to dealing with the government while other countries are all about reinforcing online transactions rather than paper work.

- More government involvement and support are needed. For example, a start-up that is short on cash or works on launching a new product/service or even an idea would really benefit from government support and involvement to protect it from illegal or monopolistic acts.
- Create government support mechanisms for hi-tech innovations. This is an essential recommendation, given the nature of the new and trending entrepreneurial businesses.
- Promote financial policy reform and stabilization, especially for interest and exchange rates. A lot of trials did not make it due to the economic instability, devaluation, high interest rates, and exchange rate fluctuations.
- Facilitate legal manners when it comes to dealing with companies that are three years old or younger.
- Provide government support for start-up participation as well as a funding mechanism program based on competitiveness rather than monopoly. If I were to start a new business, I would feel so much safer starting it in a country with a government that supports, protects, and can help protect my business in case of any drop recession in that business.
- Increase media awareness and highlight grassroot success stories. Such practices can be very inspiring and encouraging for others to kick start theirs.
- Promote and educate students about entrepreneurship at primary and secondary schools. Support innovation in learning curricula instead of memorization.
- Encourage more affordable market researches that can really be reliable and can help start-ups and MSMEs.
- Work on establishing a flexible and adequate legislative and regulatory framework to support entrepreneurship in Egypt.
- Work on digitalizing government related procurement, as discussed before, to avoid bureaucracy, bribes, and reduce the time spent on such acts.
- Ease restrictions on nongovernment organizations (NGOs) operating in the ecosystem to promote such organizations and encourage them.

- Encourage companies to start up by issuing government subsidies and running grants to help with operational overhead.
- Facilitate bank financing and loans for SMEs and start-ups. This was only done in one bank in Egypt, and it helped a lot of businesses kick start their career. However, it still needs more facilitation and to be in more than just one governmental bank. Moreover, loan amounts need to be a bit more than what is offered after calculating and weighing the risks of the proposed project.
- Adjust taxes by exempting or giving tax breaks to those who earn under a certain amount of money and applying taxes on those who perform significantly well within a small amount of time.
- De-regulate investment bureaucracy to facilitate some banned industries such as crowdfunding platforms and drones.

Following are some recommendations of policies and practices that were suggested by GEM participants to be reinforced in Egypt. It was seen that entrepreneurship in Egypt grew substantially over the past three years, and that the level of awareness and initiatives over that period was pretty noticeable, which shows that the potential in our market offers plenty of inspiration to new entrepreneurs to enter the marketplace.

1. *Position Egypt as a Hub for Entrepreneurs and Innovation*
   Egypt has the key enablers to support and help the growth of a start-up with its strong pool of talent, both technical and managerial, a large market, and a growing entrepreneurship ecosystem. All Egypt needs to become a hub for entrepreneurship and innovation are some strategies to help position it and recognize it as one. First, and as discussed briefly, there is a need for improving access to entrepreneurial finance, particularly venture capital funds and angel investors. More than $200 million of Egyptian venture capital (VC) funds were recently announced, and several regional VC funds started to target Egyptian start-ups, with a growing number of visible investments. However, there is a visible gap in VC funding for investments between $50k and $500k, which creates a high risk in losing

promising early-stage start-ups. Government needs to focus on the creation of *funds-of-funds*, supporting small early-stage funds to fill this gap. Additionally, government and development financial institution (DFI) funds should encourage Egyptian start-ups to remain located and operating in Egypt rather than registering in offshore locations or relocating to other destinations.

Second, incentives should be provided to retain and develop technical and managerial talents in Egypt. The reason Egypt can be thought to be a hub for entrepreneurship is the potential it holds whether with regard to skills and human force, on the one hand, or the technical talents and opportunities it has to offer on the other. This is in addition to the fact that despite the challenges of the educational system, Egypt still produces a strong technical and managerial talent pool. However, there is rapid brain drain in areas that relate to technical and entrepreneurial talent, whether to competing regional hubs or to multinational corporations. We need to develop strategies and incentives to retain such talents as they represent the core of any entrepreneurial ecosystem or competitive knowledge economy.

2. *Expand Entrepreneurial Education and Awareness Among Youth*

This was one of the main and most important recommendations not just for Egypt but for any developing or even developed country. Education is always the key to successful and rising economies. In our case, Egypt scores in areas such as entrepreneurial awareness, perception, and intent are among the highest globally, indicating strong aspirations, especially among youth. However, these aspirations are often not translating into actual start-ups reflecting this potential, mostly due to the limited business education among Egyptians in general.

The educational system is witnessing a radical change; however, it may take decades to see the impact of these reforms. Therefore, there has to be a scalable and cost-efficient educational tool that is accessible and attractive to the young generation, for example massive open online courses (MOOCs), social media campaigns, and embedding business educational content in mass media.

The entrepreneurial education and awareness should focus on two important factors. First, it should stress on building confidence among youth and young professionals to launch their start-ups— which works against every single norm they were raised up on such as aspiring safe jobs (governmental or large corporate jobs). This does not mean that such jobs are not needed or can be beneficial even for entrepreneurs at times. However, we can choose to make them look at the fact that these large organizations were once an idea and then a start-up themselves until they became these large entities that our parents think it is safe to work for. Instead of working in a governmental boring slow-paced job, they can shift their thinking to a new way that can help enhance the performance of such organizations and help facilitate their jobs making them more efficient and easier.

3. *Unleash the Power of Youth Entrepreneurship for Inclusive Growth and Job Creation*

   Most of the narrative around entrepreneurship is focused on *tech start-ups*, often neglecting traditional SMEs that provide the foundation for social and economic inclusion and job creation. Such type is the base in entrepreneurship in Egypt; thus, it cannot be neglected. Entrepreneurs in these areas are often young, necessity-driven, creating low-productivity enterprises in sectors such as manufacturing, retail, and agri-business. However, these SMEs provide an engine for job creation, and can easily be accelerated to faster growth and productivity. Significant progress has been achieved toward providing access to finance for SMEs. Examples are the Central Bank of Egypt (CBE) initiative to provide low-interest SME loans and the launch of new micro-finance NGOs and corporations targeting micro-enterprises. However, most of these efforts target formal businesses, with a significant part of the economy that remains informal and still does not have access to finance. Major reforms were also implemented in the areas of investment laws and industrial licensing requirements; however, micro and small enterprises remain challenged in dealing with government red tape regulations. Dealing with more than a dozen government agencies, often on weekly basis, drains the resources and energy of small enterprises, promotes informality, and impedes growth. Major administrative reforms are needed to reduce this burden and promote growth, creation, and formalization within this sector.

4. *Strengthen the Entrepreneurship Ecosystem Through Programs and Policies*

   The emerging entrepreneurship ecosystem in Egypt is promising and can have a transforming effect on economic growth and inclusion.

Expert assessments through the GEM NES acknowledge improvements, albeit limited, in areas such as access to finance, government policies, internal market dynamics, easier market entry regulations, as well as cultural and social norms. The figures indicated the beginning of a positive momentum, despite the low rankings in most of the ecosystem indicators.

Finally, it can be said that these recommendations are all important and, if reinforced and worked on, they could really help boost Egypt position in the world in the entrepreneurial sector. They should all work together in harmony as one factor affects the other and so on. Education should set the base and foundation in children's minds. Awareness would light up that dark and traditional part in everyone's mind, making them more open to either starting their own business and taking risk or to trying that new start-up they heard of that offers something merely new to what they are used to. Government intervention to help facilitate the operation of those businesses and protect them, especially those necessity-driven entrepreneurial start-ups, will be the milestone in setting Egypt as a hub for entrepreneurship ecosystem.

Conclusion

GEM is an annual assessment of the entrepreneurial activity, aspirations, and attitudes of individuals across a wide range of countries. Initiated in 1999 as a partnership between London Business School and Babson College, the first study covered 10 countries. Since then, close to 100 *National Teams* from every corner of the globe have participated in the project, which continues to grow annually. GEM is the largest ongoing study of entrepreneurial dynamics in the world. It explores the role of entrepreneurship in national economic growth, unveiling the detailed national features and characteristics associated with entrepreneurial activity. The data collected is *harmonized* by a central team of experts, guaranteeing its quality and facilitating cross-national comparisons. The program has three main objectives: to measure differences in the level of entrepreneurial activity between countries, to uncover factors leading to appropriate levels of entrepreneurship, and to suggest policies that may enhance the national level of entrepreneurial activity. GEM is unique because, unlike other entrepreneurship datasets that measure newer and smaller firms, GEM studies, at the grassroots level, the behavior of individuals with respect to starting and managing a business. This approach provides a more detailed picture of entrepreneurial activity than is found in official national registry datasets. In the GEM Working Paper Series, authors from within and outside the GEM consortium publish the results of ongoing research using GEM data for early dissemination of their research results. Papers serve to present an idea of how GEM data can be used, and may be of particular use for researchers who are new to the data.

CHAPTER 10

Reasons for Business Discontinuation

Introduction

Business discontinuation is a vital component of active economies. A mainstream of entrepreneurship literature has concentrated on efficacious endeavors. Therefore, little is known about why endeavors fail. It is complex, being both a sign of economic vitality and the source of effective individual trauma. This chapter presents a review of the literature to date. The purpose of this review is to provide a complete and serious analysis of business discontinuation research, classify the key reasons of business discontinuation, bond the gap between the numerous perspectives, and grow a consistent understanding of the phenomena upon which future studies can be based.

Start-up business as a high-risk venture may not reach the final line. Each year, many thousands of founders start their new businesses with the hope of achieving great success, but, unfortunately, small business statistics show that more than half of them fail. According to the European Association of Business Angels, about 50 million new projects (137,000 per day) are launched every year, but 90 percent of them fail. The most common reasons that cause the failure of a new project can be divided into three categories: technical, financial, and sales/marketing. In this chapter, we gather and identify the factors that lead to the failure of start-up business to provide an overview of the mistakes that founders may commit at the beginning of their business.

Business discontinuation studies have their heritage in the finance as the formation of commercial banks significantly enlarged the flow and the spread of financial data. Since then, it has been discovered and considered by a variety of researchers using different procedures. A new resurrection of interest in the topic has happened recently with an obvious and satisfying growth in studies associated with business discontinuation developing from entrepreneurship literature. The transformed awareness of business failure inside the entrepreneurship field focuses on individuals' involvement in failure, thus departing from the moderately separate methods, such as logical exhibiting, that were ordinary when the subject debuted in finance literature. Gathering information on such a delicate topic is hard. Moreover, the leaning of researchers to choose their definition based on access to data rather than logical reasoning is concerning. The purpose of this review is to discover these problems and offer a glimpse of the evolution of business discontinuation studies and key discussions that have bonded the issue along these years within entrepreneurship literature.

Among the early approaches were those of Altman (1968) and Beaver (1966) who proposed to use a firm financial data to predict its probability to fail. The first statistical models developed were based on discriminant analysis (Beaver 1966) and multiple discriminant analysis (Altman 1968), followed by more recent approaches exploiting regression (Kolari, Glennon, Shin, and Caputo 2002; Martin 1977; Zmijewski 1984). Since the 1980s, artificial intelligence methods started to be used as well to predict ventures success/failure. The suggested solutions relied on decision tree algorithms (Frydman, Altman, and Kao 1985), artificial neural networks (Tam 1991), clustering (Ozkan, Türkşen, and Canpolat 2008), and hybrid genetic algorithms (Chiam, Tan, and Mamun 2009). Approaches based on financial data had the advantage of being potentially applied to a high number of companies, as data could be gathered from their annual reports. Nonetheless, company revenues were frequently consequences of other aspects, such as entrepreneur's ability, company core competencies, market, and so on. In this view, other research works investigated whether such aspects could contribute as well to the success or failure of a venture.

According to statistics published in 2019 by the Small Business Administration (SBA), about 20 percent of business start-ups fail in the first year. About half succumb to business failure within five years. By Year 10, only about 33 percent survive. Those statistics are rather grim. In 2020, small business survival became an even bigger worry because of coronavirus-related declines in sales. While there are a multitude of conditions that can result in a business failing, most years, the reasons small companies go out of business is because they make one or more common mistakes.

Business discontinuation is defined as exiting business due to failure to sustain the business ongoing, and it is a measure of economy

Business closings hold steady while business startups decline

Business startups have been declining steadily in the U.S. over the past 30 years. But the startup rate crossed a critical threshold in 2008, when the birth rate of new businesses dropped below the death rate for the first time since these metrics were first recorded.

■ % closed firms   ▒ % new firms

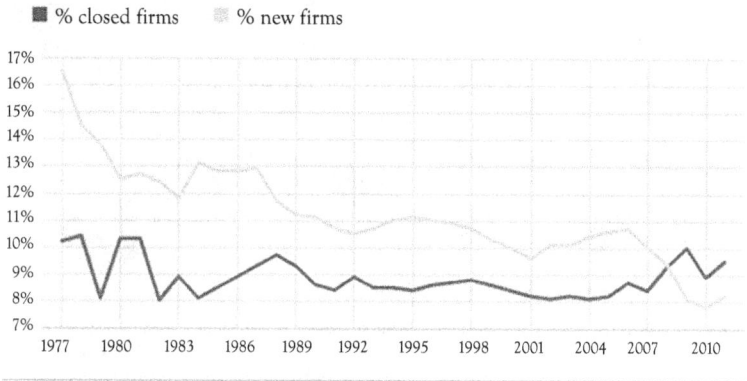

Figure 10.1 Business start-ups decline

Source: U.S. Census Bureau, Business Dynamics Statistics

strength. If the rate of business discontinuation decreases, this means that the country economy is strong and vice versa. Research indicates that the failure of SMEs is high, above all within the first year after starting (Franco and Haase 2010). Timmons (1994) show that over 20 percent of new ventures fail within the first year and 66 percent within six years. Other scholars like Paffenholz (1998) and Woywode (1998) state that approximately 50 percent of small start-ups survive for more than five years (Franco and Haase 2010). According to the GEM and Vanags (2018), in 10 economies, discontinuance rates were half or more the level of total early-stage entrepreneurial activity. Six of these were from the Middle East and Africa (Angola, Egypt, Iran, Morocco, Saudi Arabia, and Sudan); three were from Europe (Cyprus, Greece, and Sweden); and one was from Asia (Taiwan). According to Small Business Service (2001), in the UK, 350,000 to 400,000 businesses close every year—in recent years, about 10 percent of the total stock. Among high-income countries, Norway, the United States, Republic of Korea, Iceland, and Ireland have the highest rates of business discontinuation (Arasti 2011). That is why, it is very important to analyze and understand the causes of business discontinuation in order to enhance entrepreneurship and, consequently, enhance the economy.

Literature Review

American Portal CB Insights, which collects and analyzes a huge amount of data using algorithms and data visualization, compiled a ranking of the most common factors of start-up failure based on the information gathered. The survey was conducted on 101 start-ups that unfortunately could not resist the pitfalls of the start-up environment.

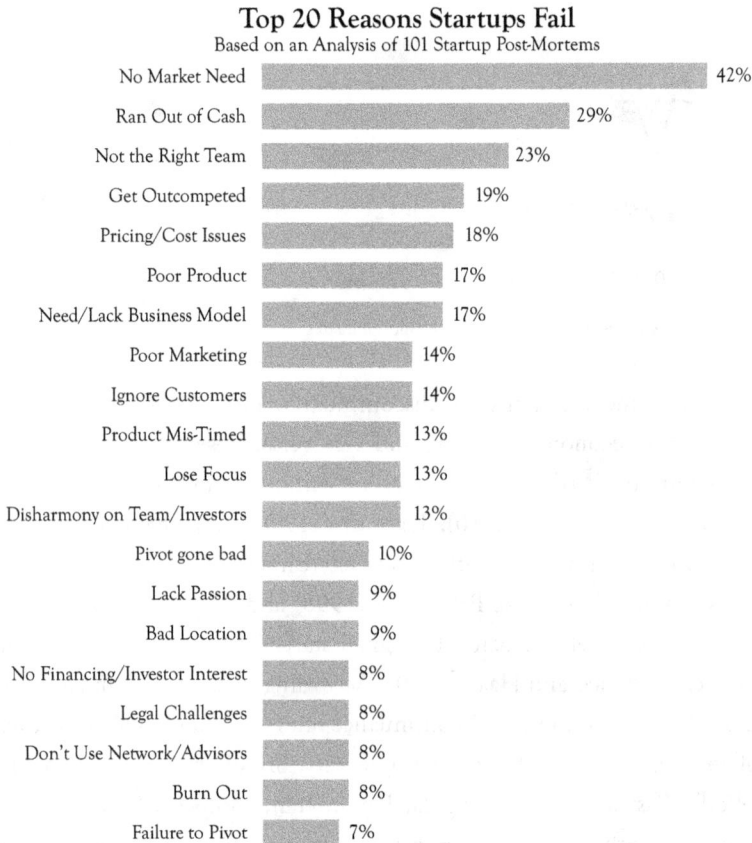

Top 20 Reasons Startups Fail
Based on an Analysis of 101 Startup Post-Mortems

Reason	Percentage
No Market Need	42%
Ran Out of Cash	29%
Not the Right Team	23%
Get Outcompeted	19%
Pricing/Cost Issues	18%
Poor Product	17%
Need/Lack Business Model	17%
Poor Marketing	14%
Ignore Customers	14%
Product Mis-Timed	13%
Lose Focus	13%
Disharmony on Team/Investors	13%
Pivot gone bad	10%
Lack Passion	9%
Bad Location	9%
No Financing/Investor Interest	8%
Legal Challenges	8%
Don't Use Network/Advisors	8%
Burn Out	8%
Failure to Pivot	7%

Figure 10.2 Business startup decline (as cited in Arnaud 2018)

No market need (42 percent): One of the biggest problems is ignoring customer interest in introducing your product or service. As a founder, you should care about the customer need and solve the problems that arise from your competitors. Founders should make a market research based on accurate information before founding the project in addition to analyzing market environment.

Ran out of cash/insufficient funds (29 percent): Finding enough financial resources is very important to the success of any start-up business, especially in the first phase of launching, as there is no generated revenue. Insufficient operating funds can cause a forced closure before having a fair chance to succeed. They also cannot expect a realistic incoming revenue from sales. Spending cash according to a strategic plan is important to avoid running out of cash.

Not the right team (23 percent): Building a wrong team is a direct reason of a start-up failure. A diverse team with different experiences can form a real threat on the success of the start-up. The founders should spread and encourage the spirit of cooperation and participation.

Get outcompeted (19 percent): Start-up founders should maintain their core competencies and keep into competition.

Pricing or cost issues (18 percent): The pricing of the product/service may be one of the main reasons of the project success as it may be a competitive advantage. Product development is complex, expensive, and almost always takes longer than anticipated. Even big tech companies developing new products always struggle to estimate the time and cost required.

Poor product (17 percent): Companies should take the value delivered by their product/service to the customer into consideration.

Lack of a business model (17 percent): It is critical for all businesses to have an accurate business plan based on well-known information. This can ease the track of success and development of any new project.

Poor marketing (14 percent): Segmentation, targeting, and positioning represent the perfect way to market a product. Good marketing based on segmentation, which targets to deliver the right product to the right customer, is one of the most important skills of a successful start-up. It also attracts attention and turns noncustomers into customers.

Ignoring customer needs (13 percent): Empirical results point toward a significant relationship between customer satisfaction and economic performance in general, but less is known about how the satisfaction of company customers translates into security pricing and investment returns, and virtually nothing is known about the associated risks. The tacit link between buyer utility and the allocation of investment capital is a fundamental principle on which the economic system of free market capitalism rests (Anderson 1996; Anderson, Fornell, and Lehmann 1994; Anderson, Fornell, and Mazvancheryl 2004)

Product mistimed (13 percent): Choosing the right time to provide the product/service to the customer, especially in the season.

Lose focus (13 percent): Focusing is very important to keep your business competitive edge.

Disharmony in the team/investors (13 percent): Without a harmonious attitude in the company between both the team and investors, there will be confusion in decisions and their implementation.

Pivot gone bad (10 percent): According to CB Insights collection of 242 start-up postmortems, approximately 10 percent of the failed startup entrepreneurs surveyed attributed their failure at least partially to a *pivot gone bad*, while 7 percent attributed it partially to a failure to pivot. These start-ups do not give the complete picture. A business that needed to pivot in the first place is a business with other, more complex problems (and motivations for failure).

Lack of passion (9 percent): Most of founders lose their passion after facing some problems and not reaching their expected targets.

Bad location (9 percent): Founders should be very careful in choosing the location that should be close to suppliers, to reduce the transportation cost, and to the customers that they target. According to SBA studies, poor location is among the chief causes of all business failures. In determining a site for a retail operation, you must be willing to pay for a good location. The cost of the location often reflects the volume and/or quality of the business you will generate.

No financing/investor interest (8 percent): One of the important entrepreneur's tasks is to keep the interest of investors to provide cash to keep the project open.

Legal challenges (8 percent): Sometimes, ignorance of some legal challenges may cause to falling in financial problems that may cause the closure of the project.

Lack of use of the network (8 percent): Every business should have a professional-looking and well-designed website that enables users to easily find out about their business and how to avail themselves of their products and services. In the United States alone, there were 312 million Internet users in 2019, and the U.S. Census Bureau estimates e-commerce sales were $601.7 billion (Clement October 02, 2020).

Cash burnout (8 percent): Taking the right decision to cut your losses and redirect your efforts at the critical point before failure to avoid burnout.

Failure to pivot (8 percent): You should know the perfect time to switch to another product or another strategy.

According to Michael Ames (1983), the major reasons for small business failure are (1) lack of experience, (2) insufficient capital (money), (3) poor location, (4) poor inventory management, (5) overinvestment in fixed assets, (6) poor credit arrangement management, (7) personal use of business funds, (8) unexpected growth. In addition, according to Gustav Berle (1989), there are two more reasons: (9) competition, (10) low sales. Moreover, according to Patricia Schaefer (2020), the top eight reasons for business failure are:

1. *You Start Your Business for the Wrong Reasons*
   The desire to make a lot of money, hope of having more time with one's family, or being on one's own—benefits that some successful entrepreneurs achieve after years of hard work—are not reasons to start a business. The right reasons for starting a business and building a successful company include the following:

- You have a passion for what you will be doing.
- You strongly believe—based on educated study and investigation—that your product or service would fulfill a real need in the marketplace.
- You are very determined.
- Failures do not defeat you. You learn from your mistakes and use these lessons as business tips to help you succeed the next time around.
- You thrive on independence and are skilled at taking charge when a creative or intelligent solution is needed.
- You get along with and can deal with all different types of individuals.

2. *There Is No Market or Too Small of a Market*

   Before you start a business, you need to determine if there is a market for what you plan to sell and if that market is big enough to be profitable. Keep in mind that not *everyone* is a market. To avoid business failure after start-up, business owners should keep an eye on their market and customer changing needs.

3. *Poor Management*

   Poor management is the number one reason for failure. New business owners frequently lack relevant business and management expertise in areas such as finance, purchasing, selling, production as well as hiring and managing employees. If the business owner does not recognize what they do not do well and seek help, the company may fail and go out of business. To fix the problem, small business owners can educate themselves on skills they lack, hire skilled employees, or outsource work to capable professionals.

4. *Insufficient Capital*

   Novel business owners often do not understand cash flow and underestimate how much money they will need to get the business started. As a result, they are forced to close before they have had a fair chance to succeed. They also may have an unrealistic expectation of incoming revenues from sales. It is imperative to determine how much money your business will require. You need to know not only the costs of starting your business but also the costs of staying in business. It is important to realize that many businesses take a year or two to get going. You need enough funds to cover all costs until sales can finally pay for these costs.

5. *Wrong Location*

Location is critical to the success of most local businesses. A bad location could spell disaster to even the best-managed enterprise. Some factors to consider are:

- Where your customers are
- Traffic, accessibility, parking, and lighting
- Warehousing or equipment storage needs
- Location of competitors
- Condition and safety of the building
- Local incentive programs for business start-ups in specific targeted areas
- History, community flavor and receptiveness to a new business at a prospective site

If you usually do not have customers or clients entering your business establishment, the ideal location for your start-up could be your own home.

6. *Lack of Planning*

It is critical for all businesses to have a business plan, and it must be realistic and based on accurate, current information and educated projections for the future. Components should include:

- Description of the business, vision, goals and keys to success
- Market analysis
- Workforce needs
- Potential problems and solutions
- Financial considerations: capital equipment and supply list, balance sheet, income statement and cash flow analysis, sales and expense forecast
- Competitive analysis
- Marketing, advertising, and promotional activities
- Budgeting and managing company growth

In addition, most bankers request a business plan if you are seeking funds.

7. *Overexpansion*

Overexpansion often happens when business owners confuse success with how fast they can expand their business. A focus on slow and steady growth is optimum. Many a bankruptcy has been caused by rapidly expanding companies. At the same time, you do not want to limit growth. Once you have an established solid customer base and a good cash flow, let your success help you set the right measured pace.

8. *No Website and No Social Media Presence*

You need a website and social media presence. Every business should have a professional-looking and well-designed website that enables users to easily find out about their business and how to benefit themselves of their products and services. If you serve local customers, your website should include your address, phone number, and working hours. It should be listed in *Google My Business* so that it can show up when customers search for what you sell by location. You get most of your business through networking and referrals. You need a website so that potential customers can research your business before they call you. If you have products that can be sold online, or you can take orders online, that is an added benefit. Nevertheless, at the basic minimum, you need a website that lets customers know what you offer and how they benefit by doing business with you.

According to Zhang et al. (2020), the common reasons of businesses failure are:

9. *Starting With Too Much Debt*

Sometimes, it is necessary to go into debt to finance the launch or purchase of your business. Few aspiring business owners don't have the cash to pay out of pocket, so loans are a reasonable choice to help finance a new venture. However, if you do not prioritize repaying your debt and making timely payments, it becomes harder to grow operations. Small business owners through all industries report that lacking of capital or cash flow is their highest challenge. Adding the load of debt makes it more difficult to reach profit. To avoid starting out with so much debt to repay, you may think about alternative funding methods.

REASONS FOR BUSINESS DISCONTINUATION 103

10. *No Business Plan*

A business plan is a crucial element for a small business. Your business plan will help you with almost all aspects of your business, from financing to operations. If you create your business plan early on, you can use it as a guide and a checklist throughout your small business journey. With a good business plan, you will research and understand key areas for success.

11. *Mismanaged Cash Flow*

Cash flow and profit are two different things. You can be profitable but still not have cash. Profit looks at the current state of your sales—including sales that may have not been processed with your accounts receivable yet. Ignoring your cash flow means ignoring the money you actually have to work with. You need that cash for daily operational needs like paying invoices, bills, and employees. As a business is growing, it is important that accounts receivable be managed to focus on cash flow. When companies fail to make adjustments to cash flow while they are growing, it is more likely they will run out of operating capital. if you are out of capital, it is almost impossible to keep ahead of invoices and paying employees.

12. *Ineffective Leadership*

Active listening, empathy, encouragement, communication, and compromise are skills that should be considered to step into a leadership role. As a business owner, your employees, vendors, and clients will all look to you as a reflection of the business as a whole.

13. *Failure to Adapt*

New or adjusted business models have kept many businesses running during times of no or limited in-person occupancy. Change is a constant, so it can be dangerous to grow satisfied. Even if things are going well with your business at the moment, being unprepared or unwilling to adjust can be dangerous. Regularly looking to improve your processes, tweak your business model, and innovate your product or services all help you prepare for future success and protect against future change.

According to Mike Kamo (2020), there are six reasons your small business will fail:

1. *Leadership Failure*

   Your business will fail if you show poor management skills. You will struggle as a leader if you do not have enough experience making management decisions, supervising a staff, or the vision to lead your organization.

2. *Lacking Uniqueness and Value*

   You may have a good product or your service has strong demand, but your business is still failing. May be your approach is mediocre, or you do not have a strong value proposition. If there is strong demand, you probably have many competitors, and it is hard to stand out in the crowd.

3. *Not in Touch With Customer Needs*

   Keep in touch with your customers and understand what they need. Keep an eye on the feedback they offer. Your customers may like your product or service, but they might love it if you changed a feature or altered a procedure.

4. *Unprofitable Business Model*

   Similar to leadership failure is building a company on a business model that is not sound, operating without a business plan, or pursuing a business for which there is no proven revenue stream. The business idea may be great, but you may fail in the implementation of the idea.

5. *Poor Financial Management*

   Your business can fail if you lack a contingency funding plan, a reserve of money you can call upon in the event of a financial crisis. Occasionally, people start businesses with a dream of making money, but they do not have skills to manage cash flow, taxes, expenses, and other financial matters. Poor accounting practice pushes a business to failure.

6. *Rapid Growth and Overexpansion*

   Every now and then, a business start-up grows much faster than it can keep up with. You start a website with a trending product and, unexpectedly, you are asked for orders you are not able to fulfill. On the other hand, perhaps the opposite is true. You are convinced that your product is going to succeed that you invest much and order too much inventory, but you cannot move it.

According to Garfield, Moore, and Adams (2019), there are ten reasons why seven out of 10 businesses fail within 10 years:

1. *Failure to Deliver Real Value*

   Value is the heart of any business. The world most successful businesses deliver the highest value. They always overdeliver, no matter what the situation is. If you are looking to get rich quick, you will quickly fail. Instead, focus on the real value proposition, adding more value than your competitors do.

2. *Failure to Connect With the Target Audience*

   If you do not connect with your target audience, your business will fail. You have to be aware of your potential consumers' wants and needs.

3. *Failure to Optimize Conversions*

   Conversion rate optimization (CRO) is a system for increasing the percentage of visitors to a website that convert into customers, or more generally, take any desired action on a webpage. Without optimizing conversions, no matter what a business does, especially if it raises money and has a high burn rate, it will be useless trying to survive when money runs out. Address the conversions early on to ensure that there is a positive return on investment (ROI). Therefore, you know you have a sustainable business.

4. *Failure to Create an Effective Sales Funnel*

   The sales funnel is each step that someone has to take in order to become your customer. Building an effective sales funnel should be one of the primary goals of any founder. These automated selling machines help to reduce friction in making the sale and help to put many of the functions of running a business on autopilot, allowing founders to grow things like traffic sources or to educate consumers through webinars and so on. Sales funnels also help to build a relationship with the consumer through e-mail warming campaigns.

5. *Lack of Authenticity and Transparency*

   Businesses that lack authenticity and transparency will fail one day soon. Without customers' needs in sight and a focus on the wrong things, businesses could easily lose consumers' trust. Rather than risking that, focus on being authentic, transparent, and finding ways that you can give more rather than take.

6. *Unable to Compete Against Market Leaders*

Staying afloat is exponentially harder when competition is severe, especially true in profitable markets where the stakes are high. If smaller businesses cannot compete against their larger counterparts, they need to find ways to pivot and stay in business. To do that takes a keen business sense and true guts.

7. *Inability to Control Expenses*

It is easy to spend when funds are available. However, having a critical sense to control company expenses is mandatory. When expenses get out of control, it is impossible for a business to survive.

8. *Lack of Strategic and Effective Leadership*

Most businesses lack strategic and effective leadership. Without real experience in the business world, most newcomers to the entrepreneurial arena struggle with the irresistible amount of demands placed on them when problems do arise.

9. *Failure to Build an Employee "Tribe"*

Your employee tribe and culture are crucial for long-term success. Most businesses will fail because they forget about their employees.

10. *Failure to Create Proper Business Systems*

Customer relationship management (CRM) needs to be implemented and customized. Policies need to take place. Financial audits and tracking procedures need to be created. Without good systems and automation, the amount of work becomes too hard, and the details can easily be missed.

Conclusion

Business discontinuation is an ubiquitous danger for numerous business visionaries. It could be a theme that warrants cautious thought by entrepreneurship analysts. However, both trade history specialists and administration researchers contend to date have basically concentrated on considering victory cases and paid generally small consideration to firm disappointment. Failure may be a result of factors from both outside and inside the organization. Maybe one or two factors occur simultaneously. Business research is the most important step before launching your business to know the market real need. Ignoring receiving product feedback and criticism causes also the failure of founders to continue in the market. It is essential to realize that buyer and user satisfaction are the main targets of business success. In addition, one of the common factors of start-up failure may be incorrect timing. Some start-ups launch products ignoring that the right technology is not yet available. Financial considerations and cash funds are a very important factor in the success and continuity of a business, but it should be based on good planning. Spending cash according to a strategic plan to avoid running out of cash is essential. Without a harmonious attitude in the company between both the team and investors, there will be confusion in decisions and their implementation. Good marketing based on segmentation targeting and positioning is yet another important consideration. You should choose a perfect location that serves the project and your targeted customer. As a founder of a business, you should take all the aforementioned points, and other issues like EGO, theatrical reality, uncontrolled growth, lack of experience, and so on into consideration to avoid failure or discontinuity of your project.

CHAPTER 11

A Case Study

Doing Business in Egypt With the Benchmarks of the Other Middle East Countries

Basic Research

Doing Business in Egypt 2020

Overview

Doing Business 2020 is the 17th in a series of annual studies measuring the regulations that improve business activity and those that constrain it. *Doing Business* presents quantitative indicators on business regulations and the protection of property rights that can be compared across 190 economies—including Egypt—and over time. It covers 10 areas of business regulation: starting a business, dealing with construction permits, getting electricity, registering property, getting credit, protecting minority investors, paying taxes, trading across borders, enforcing contracts, and resolving insolvency. By documenting changes in regulations across 10 areas of business activity in 190 economies, *Doing Business* analyzes regulations that encourage efficiency and support freedom to do business.

The data collected by *Doing Business* addresses three questions about government. First, when do governments change regulations with a view to developing their private sector? Second, what are the characteristics of reformist governments? Third, what are the effects of regulatory change on different aspects of economic or investment activity? Answering these questions adds to our knowledge of development.

The score of each area of business regulation can be calculated by certain measurable items. The following detailed figure illustrates how exactly the scores were calculated:

1	Starting a business (rank 90)	Procedures (number) 5.5
	Score of starting a business (0–100) 87.8	Time (days) 12.5
		Cost (number) 20.3
		Paid-in minimum capital (% of income per capita) 0.0
2	Dealing with construction permits (rank 74)	Procedures (number) 20
	Score of dealing with construction permits (0–100) 71.2	Time (days) 173
		Cost (% of warehouse value) 1.3
		Building quality control index (0–15) 14.0
3	Getting electricity (rank 77)	Procedures (number) 5
	Score of getting electricity (0–100) 77.9	Time (days) 53
		Cost (% of income per capita) 180.2
		Reliability of supply and transparency of tariff index (0–8) 5
4	Registering property (rank 130)	Procedures (number) 9
	Score of registering property (0–100) 55.0	Time (days) 76
		Cost (% of property value) 1.1
		Quality of the land administration index (0–30) 9.0
5	Getting credit (rank 67)	Strength of legal rights index (0–12) 5
	Score of getting credit (0–100) 65.0	Depth of credit information index (0–8) 8
		Credit registry coverage (% of adults) 9.5
		Credit bureau coverage (% of adults) 31.3

6	Protecting minority investors (rank 57)	Extent of disclosure index (0–10) 8.0
	Score of protecting minority investors (0–100) 64.0	Extent of director liability index (0–10) 3.0
		Ease of shareholder suits index (0–10) 3.0
		Extent of shareholder right index (0–6) 6.0
		Extent of ownership and control index (0–7) 6.0
		Extent of corporate transparency index (0–7) 6.0
7	Paying taxes (rank 156)	Payments (number per year) 27
	Score of paying taxes (0–100) 55.1	Time (hours per year) 370
		Total tax and contribution rate (% of profit) 44.4
		Postfiling index (0–100) 36.3
8	Trading across borders (rank 171)	*Time to export*
	Score of trading across borders (0–100) 42.2	Documentary compliance (hours) 88
		Border compliance (hours) 48
		Cost to export
		Documentary compliance (USD) 100
		Border compliance (USD) 258
		Time to export
		Documentary compliance (hours) 265
		Border compliance (hours) 240
		Cost to export
		Documentary compliance (USD) 1,000
		Border compliance (USD) 554

(Continued)

9	Enforcing contracts (rank 166)	Time (days) 1,010
	Score of enforcing contracts (0–100) 40.0	Cost (% of claim value) 26.2
		Quality of judicial processes index (0–18) 4.0
10	Resolving insolvency (rank 104)	Recovery rate (cents on the dollar) 23.3
	Score of resolving insolvency (0–100) 42.2	Time (years) 2.5
		Cost (% of estate) 22.0
		Outcome (0 as piecemeal sale and 1 as going concern)

1. Starting a Business

Definition

This topic measures the number of procedures, time, cost, and paid-in minimum capital requirement for a small to medium-sized limited liability company to start up and formally operate in each economy largest business city.

Indicators

Procedure—men (number), time—men (days), cost—men (percent of income per capita), paid-in min. capital (percent of income per capita) (APPLIES TO BOTH MEN AND WOMEN).

Procedures

Obtain husband's permission to leave home (APPLIES TO WOMEN ONLY), submit documents, pay the fees, receive the certificate of incorporation and tax card, and four other procedures.

Score and Rank

Score: 87.7

Rank of Egypt: 90 (above average, below Tunisia and KSA, above Jordan and Lebanon)

Recommendations for Starting a Business

From 2008 till 2020, Egypt has been working to boost its performance in starting business, yet there is still room for more improvement through enhancing time and cost. However, main efforts should be made to minimize the producers (through online or one stop shop).

2. Dealing With Construction Permits

Definition
This topic tracks the procedures, time, and cost to build a warehouse, including obtaining necessary permits, submitting all required notifications, requesting and receiving all necessary inspections, and obtaining utility connections.

Indicators
Procedures (number), time (days), cost (percent of warehouse value), and building quality control index (0–15) in STANDERDIZED WAREHOUSE.

Procedures
Apply for the site validity certificate, receive on-site inspection from the municipality, obtain site validity certificate from the municipality, obtain a geotechnical study/soil test, request, and obtain building permit from the municipality and other 16 processes.

Score and Rank
Score: 71.2
Rank of Egypt: 74 (above average, below Tunisia and KSA , above Jordan and Lebanon)

Recommendation for Dealing With Construction Permits
Almost eight months and 20 steps of producers are needed to get construction permits, but this is still all right considering the cost and building quality control index.

3. Getting Electricity

Definition
This topic measures the procedures, time, and cost required for a business to obtain a permanent electricity connection for a newly constructed warehouse.

Indicators
Procedures (number), time (days), cost (percent of income per capita), and reliability of supply and transparency of tariff index (0–8) in STANDARDIZED CONNECTION.

Procedures
Submit application to SCEDC and await estimate, obtain external inspection, and estimate of connection fees from SCEDC, and other three procedures.

Score and Rank
Score: 77.9
Rank of Egypt: 77 (above average, below Tunisia, KSA and Jordan, above Lebanon)

Recommendation for Getting Electricity
Getting electricity in Egypt can be done in five procedures within about two months, but Egypt has an issue in reliability of supply and transparency of tariff Index. It could be fixed by clearly setting regulatory monitoring of utility performance and setting a fair price of electricity.

4. Registering Property

Definition
This topic examines the steps, time, and cost involved in registering property, assuming a standardized case of an entrepreneur who wants to purchase land and a building that is already registered and is free of title dispute.

Indicators
Procedures (number), time (days), cost (percent of property value), and quality of the land administration index (0–30).

Procedures
Obtain property tax statement from the Tax Authority, check for encumbrances at the District Land Registry, and seven other procedures.

Score and Rank
Score: 55

Rank of Egypt: 130 (below average, below Tunisia, KSA, Jordan and Lebanon)

Recommendation for Registering Property
In comparison to other countries, Egypt is extremely affected because of the registration producers and quality of land administration index, so the recommendation here is to increase the efficacy to have clear geographic coverage index and avoid land dispute.

5. Getting Credit

Definition
This topic explores two sets of issues, namely the strength of credit reporting systems and the effectiveness of collateral and bankruptcy laws in facilitating lending.

Indicators
Strength of legal rights index (0–12), depth of credit information index (0–8), credit registry coverage (percent of adults), and credit bureau coverage (percent of adults). Strength of legal rights index (0–12): detailed questionnaire, each question scored by 1.

Score and Rank
Score: 65.0
Rank of Egypt: 67 (above average, below Jordan, above KSA, Tunisia and Lebanon)

Recommendation for Getting Credits
Egypt has good facilities with respect to getting credit. There is just a need to work on increasing the number of individuals and firms listed in the credit registry as a percentage of adult population to get better credit registry coverage (percent of adults).

6. Protecting Minority Investors

Definition
This topic measures the strength of minority shareholder protection against misuse of corporate assets by directors to achieve personal gain as well as shareholder rights, governance safeguards, and corporate transparency requirements that reduce the risk of abuse.

Indicators
Extent of disclosure index, extent of director liability index (0–10), ease of shareholder suits index (0–10), extent of shareholder rights index (0–6), extent of ownership and control index (0–7), extent of corporate transparency index (0–7).

Score and Rank
Score: 64.0
Rank of Egypt: 57 (above average, below KSA, above Tunisia, Jordan, and Lebanon)

Recommendation for Protecting Minority Investors
To enhance Egypt score, we need to focus on having better access to internal corporate documents, evidence obtainable during trial, and allocation of legal expenses. This is in addition to the ability of minority shareholders to sue and hold interested directors liable to prejudicial related-party transactions. By these two points, we can help enhance the protection of minority investors.
Available legal remedies: Disgorgement of profits, disqualification from managerial position(s) for one year or more, rescission of the transaction.

7. Paying Taxes

Definition
This topic records the taxes and mandatory contributions that a medium-sized company must pay or withhold in a given year, as well as the administrative burden of paying taxes and contributions and complying with postfiling procedures (VAT refund and tax audit).

Indicators
Payments (number per year), time (hours per year), total tax and contribution rate (percent of profit), and postfiling index (0–100).

Taxes by Type
Profit tax (percent of profit), labor tax and contributions (percent of profit), and other taxes (percent of profit).

Score and Rank
Score: 55.1

Rank of Egypt: 156 (below average, below KSA, Jordan, Tunisia, and Lebanon).

8. Trading Across Borders

Definition
This topic records the time and cost associated with the logistical process of exporting and importing goods.

Indicators
Time to export: border compliance (hours), cost to export: border compliance (USD), time to export: documentary compliance (hours), cost to export: documentary compliance (USD), time to import: border compliance (hours), cost to import: border compliance (USD), time to import: documentary compliance (hours), cost to import: documentary compliance (USD).

Procedures
Based on the mentioned indicators, we can go beyond the factor of importation and exportation.

Score and Rank
Score: 42.2
Rank of Egypt: 171 (below average, below Jordan, KSA, Tunisia, and Lebanon).

Recommendation for Trading Across Borders
Import is as important as export. Open markets attract investors to do business and enhance the relation between countries. In Egypt, there is a big issue with regard to the time and cost for documentary and border for both import and export, but the worst case is in time and cost to import: documentary compliance, and time to import: border compliance.

9. Enforcing Contracts

Definition
The enforcing contracts indicator measures the time and cost for resolving a commercial dispute through a local first-instance court and the quality of judicial processes index. It evaluates whether each

economy has adopted a series of good practices that promote quality and efficiency in the court system.

Indicators
Time (days), cost (percent of claim value), and quality of judicial processes index (0–18).
Quality of judicial processes index (0–18): court structure and proceedings (1–5), case management (0–6), court automation (0–4), and alternative dispute resolution (0–3).

Score and Rank
Score: 40.0
Rank of Egypt: 166 (below average, below KSA, Tunisia, Jordan, and Lebanon).

Recommendation for Enforcing Contracts
Enforcing contracts is a very important factor for resolving commercial disputes through a local court, and the quality of judicial processes index evaluates whether each economy has adopted a series of good practices that promote quality and efficiency in the court system. Egypt has time and quality of judicial process issue in addition to zero court automation, so the government needs to enhance and upgrade the score and rank and to be more attractive for doing business.

10. Resolving Insolvency

Definition
This topic studies the time, cost, and outcome of insolvency proceedings involving domestic legal entities. These variables are used to calculate the recovery rate, which is recorded as cents on the dollar recovered by secured creditors through reorganization, liquidation, or debt enforcement (foreclosure or receivership) proceedings.

Indicators
Recovery rate (cents on the dollar), time (years), cost (percent of estate), outcome (0 as piecemeal sale and 1 as going concern), and strength of insolvency framework index (0–16).

Quality measures index (0–18): Commencement of proceedings index (0–3), management of debtor's assets index (0–6), reorganization proceedings index (0–3), and creditor participation index (0–4).

Score and Rank
Score: 42.2
Rank of Egypt: 104 (above average, above Jordan, and Lebanon and KSA, below Tunisia).

Recommendations for Resolving Insolvency
Egypt has low recovery rate and reorganization proceedings index but moderate strength of insolvency framework index, so economic leaders have to work on improving the outcome of business and the present value of debt recovered.

Extra Measurable Item: Employing Workers

The indicators measure hiring , working hours, redundancy rules, and redundancy cost.
The study does not present rankings of economies with regard to these indicators nor include the topic in the aggregate ease of doing business score or ranking.
Doing Business 2020 reforms making it easier to do business in the following factors.

Factors Necessary for Enhancing Egypt Rank and Business Doing

1. *Encouraging an Economic Environment*
    The government should focus on enhancing market stability and potential for growth. In addition, steady GDP growth shows that consumer expenditure has been growing steadily over the years, and it shows no signs of getting down. This makes it an ideal place for you to ride on this trend of economic success. Moreover, the government considers being both willing and able to support entrepreneurship and trade. It has usually offered strong infrastructural support for such activities, mentoring, and low-cost legal advice for proprietors

to structure and manage their businesses. Essentially, among other benefits for businesses, this means that no tariffs will be placed on exports and imports.

2. *Straightforward Legal Requests*

There is no need to worry about being bogged down by unnecessary administration and legal restrictions when it comes to starting a business. Slightly different regulations may apply to each individual, depending on which business is being started. Some of these procedures involve registering to pay the goods and services tax or registering as an employer in order to be able to operate the business. However, paperwork to set up a business can be completed online with much ease and convenience.

3. *A Supportive Start-Up Community*

You will need all the care you can get when you dive head first into opening a business. That is why, it is significant to have a community with resources that you can tap on. You need to find no absence whenever you need advice, a listening ear, or just someone to share ideas with.

4. *A Flexible Tax System*

Tax is one of the inescapable actualities of life. For small businesses, tax often is a concern given how it impacts the company income. The tax environment should be relatively flexible or include discount on taxes for individuals in self-employed positions or in partnerships as well as a number of rebates for sole trader and partners.

Economy Profile of the Arab Republic of Egypt

By *Doing Business 2020*

The *Doing Business* project, launched in 2002, looks at domestic small and medium-sized companies and measures the regulations applying to them through their life cycle. It provides objective measures of business regulations and their enforcement across 190 economies and selected cities at the subnational and regional level.

This study is specifically focusing on four main countries in the neighborhood: KSA, Jordan, Lebanon, and Tunisia to compare with in addition to the fourth comparative, which is the region average (Middle East and North Africa). The analysis is done by gathering and analyzing comprehensive quantitative data to compare business regulation environments across economies and over time.

The data collected for comparison can lead the reader to a conclusion that is very benefitable in taking a decision related to business startups or even regarding investment in a company already doing business. The data gives us the following indicators (with ranks and scores):

Starting a Business: Procedures, time, cost, and paid-in minimum capital to start a limited liability company

Dealing with Construction Permits: Procedures, time, and cost to complete all formalities to build a warehouse, and the quality control and safety mechanisms in the construction permitting system

Getting Electricity: Procedures, time, and cost to get connected to the electrical grid, and the reliability of the electricity supply and the transparency of tariffs

Registering Property: Procedures, time, and cost to transfer a property and the quality of the land administration system

Getting Credit: Movable collateral laws and credit information systems

Protecting Minority Investors: Minority shareholders' rights in related-party transactions and in corporate governance

Paying Taxes: Payments, time, total tax, and contribution rate for a firm to comply with all tax regulations as well as postfiling processes

Trading Across Borders: Time and cost to export the product of comparative advantage and import auto parts

Enforcing Contracts: Time and cost to resolve a commercial dispute and the quality of judicial processes

Resolving Insolvency: Time, cost, outcome, and recovery rate for a commercial insolvency and the strength of the legal framework for insolvency

Economy Profile of the Arab Republic of Egypt Benchmarking With Other Arabic Countries

By *Doing Business 2020*

Rank	Egypt	KSA	Jordon	Lebanon	Tunisia	Average (Middle East and North Africa)
Starting business	90	38	120	151	19	
Dealing with construction permits	74	28	138	164	32	
Getting electricity	77	18	69	127	63	
Registering property	130	19	78	110	94	
Getting credit	67	80	4	132	104	
Protecting minority investors	57	3	105	114	61	
Paying taxes	156	57	62	116	108	
Trading across borders	171	86	75	153	90	
Enforcing contracts	166	51	110	131	88	
Resolving insolvency	104	168	112	151	69	

Score	Egypt	KSA	Jordon	Lebanon	Tunisia	Average (Middle East and North Africa)
Starting business	87.8	93.1	84.5	78.2	94.6	84
Dealing with construction permits	71.2	78.3	60.3	53.7	77.4	61.7
Getting electricity	77.9	91.8	80.5	62.7	82.3	72.4
Registering property	55	84.5	66.4	59.4	63.7	63.7
Getting credit	65	60	95	40	50	41.8
Protecting minority investors	64	86	50	44	62	51.9
Paying taxes	55.1	80.5	78.7	67.5	69.4	75.1
Trading across borders	42.2	76	79	57.9	74.6	61.8
Enforcing contracts	40	65.3	55.6	50.8	58.4	56
Resolving insolvency	42.2	0	39.7	29.1	54.2	34.5

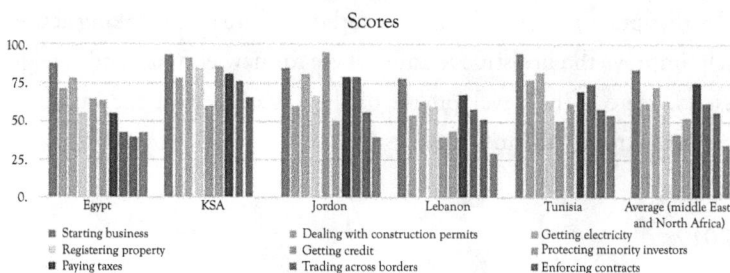

Figure 11.1 Top scores

If we sum up the total score for each country, we will find that Egypt comes in the fifth position.

Country	Egypt	KSA	Jordon	Lebanon	Tunisia	Average (Middle East and North Africa)
Total Score	600.4	715.5	689.7	543.3	686.6	602.9

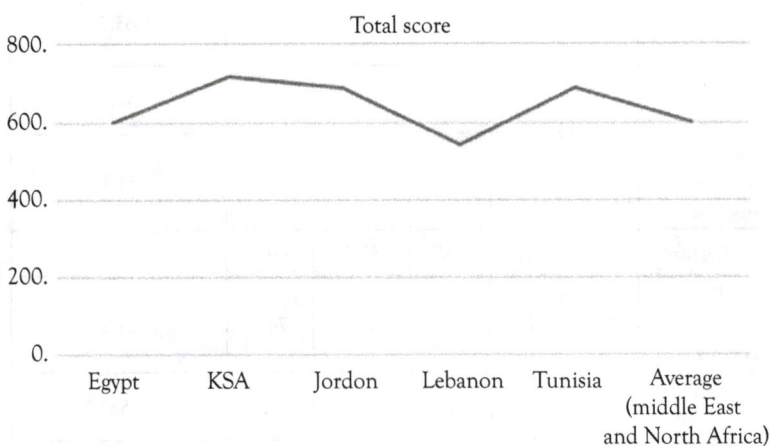

Figure 11.2 Total scores

The Egyptian government and its authorities are always taking action to help improve the investment atmosphere for new entrants and foreign investors. Here is the development of the situation with the improvements made from 2017 to 2020.

In 2017

Starting a Business

The Arab Republic of Egypt made starting a business easier by merging procedures at the one-stop shop by introducing a follow-up unit in charge of liaising with the tax and labor authority on behalf of the company.

Protecting Minority Investors

The Arab Republic of Egypt strengthened minority investor protections by increasing shareholder rights and role in major corporate decisions and by clarifying ownership and control structures.

Trading Across Borders

The Arab Republic of Egypt made trading across borders more difficult by making the process of obtaining and processing documents more complex and by imposing a cap on foreign exchange deposits and withdrawals for imports.

In 2018

Registering Property

The Arab Republic of Egypt made it more difficult to register property by raising the cost to verify and ratify a sales contract.

Protecting Minority Investors

The Arab Republic of Egypt strengthened minority investor protections by increasing shareholder rights and role in major corporate decisions.

In 2019

Starting a Business

The Arab Republic of Egypt made starting a business easier by removing the requirement to obtain a bank certificate and establishing a one-stop shop.

Getting Credit

The Arab Republic of Egypt strengthened access to credit by introducing the possibility of granting a nonpossessory security right in a single category of movable assets without requiring a specific description of the collateral. Secured creditors are now given absolute priority over other claims such as labor and tax, both outside and within bankruptcy proceedings.

Protecting Minority Investors

The Arab Republic of Egypt strengthened minority investor protections by increasing corporate transparency.

Paying Taxes

The Arab Republic of Egypt made paying taxes easier by extending value-added tax cash refunds to manufacturers in case of a capital investment.

Resolving Insolvency

The Arab Republic of Egypt made resolving insolvency easier by allowing debtors to initiate the reorganization procedure and granting creditors greater participation in the proceedings.

In 2020

Starting a Business

The Arab Republic of Egypt made starting a business easier by abolishing the requirement to obtain a certificate of nonconfusion and improving its one-stop shop.

Getting Electricity

The Arab Republic of Egypt improved the reliability of electricity supply by implementing automated systems to monitor and report power outages.

Protecting Minority Investors

The Arab Republic of Egypt strengthened minority investor protections by requiring shareholder approval when listed companies issue new shares.

Paying Taxes

The Arab Republic of Egypt made paying taxes easier by introducing an online system for filing and payment of corporate income tax and value-added tax.

About the Doing Business Organization

The project, launched in 2002, looks at domestic small and medium-sized companies and measures the regulations applying to them throughout their life cycle.

By gathering and analyzing comprehensive quantitative data to compare business regulation environments across economies and over time, *Doing Business* encourages economies to compete toward more efficient regulations, offers measurable benchmarks for reform, and serves as a resource for academics, journalists, private sector, researchers, and others interested in the business climate of each economy.

From May 2, 2018 to May 1, 2019, 115 economies implemented 294 business regulatory reforms across the 10 areas measured by *Doing Business*. Reforms inspired by *Doing Business* have been implemented by economies in all regions. The following are reforms implemented since *Doing Business* 2008.

Criteria of Evaluating Small and Medium-Sized Companies and Measuring the Regulations Applying to Them

Doing Business captures several important dimensions of the regulatory environment as they apply to local firms.

It provides quantitative indicators on the regulations for starting a business dealing with construction permits, getting electricity, registering property, getting credit, protecting minority investors, paying taxes, trading across borders, enforcing contracts, and resolving insolvency.

1. Starting a Business

This indicator measures the number of procedures, time, cost, and paid-in minimum capital requirement for a small to medium-sized limited liability company to start up and formally operate in each economy largest business city.

It uses a standardized business that is 100 percent domestically owned, has start-up capital equivalent to 10 times the income per capita, engages in general industrial or commercial activities, and employs between 10 and 50 people one month after the commencement of operations—all of whom are domestic nationals.

The business does not perform foreign trade activities and does not handle products subject to a special tax regime, for example, liquor or tobacco. It does not use heavily polluting production processes (ecosystem).

2. Dealing With Construction Permits

This indicator measures the procedures to legally build a warehouse (number), the time required to complete each procedure (calendar days), and the cost required to complete each procedure (percent of income per capita).

The dealing with construction permits indicator measures the building quality control index, evaluating the quality of building regulations; the strength of quality control and safety mechanisms; liability and insurance regimes; and professional certification requirements.

3. Getting Electricity

This indicator measures the procedures to obtain an electricity connection (number), the time required to complete each procedure (calendar days), and cost required to complete each procedure (percent of income per capita).

Additionally, the reliability of supply and transparency of tariffs index measures the reliability of supply, transparency of tariffs, and the price of electricity.

4. Registering Property

This indicator examines the steps, time, and cost involved in registering property assuming a standardized case of an entrepreneur who wants to purchase land and a building that is already registered and free of title dispute. It also measures the quality of the land administration system in each economy.

5. Getting Credit

This indicator explores two sets of issues: the strength of credit reporting systems and the effectiveness of collateral and bankruptcy laws in facilitating lending.

6. Protecting Minority Investors

This indicator measures the strength of minority shareholder protections against misuse of corporate assets by directors for their personal gain as well as shareholder rights.

7. Paying Taxes

This indicator records taxes and mandatory contributions that a medium-sized company must pay or withhold in a given year, as well as the administrative burden of paying taxes and contributions and complying with postfiling procedures (VAT refund and tax audit).

8. Trading Across Borders

This indicator measures the time and cost (excluding tariffs) associated with three sets of procedures—documentary compliance, border compliance, and domestic transport within the overall process of exporting or importing a shipment of goods.

9. Enforcing Contracts

This indicator measures the time and cost for resolving a commercial dispute through a local first-instance court and the quality of judicial processes index. It evaluates whether each economy has adopted a series of good practices that promote quality and efficiency in the court system.

10. Resolving Insolvency

This indicator studies the time, cost, and outcome of insolvency proceedings involving domestic legal entities.

These variables are used to calculate the recovery rate, which is recorded as cents on the dollar recovered by secured creditors through reorganization, liquidation, or debt enforcement to determine the present value of the amount recovered by creditors.

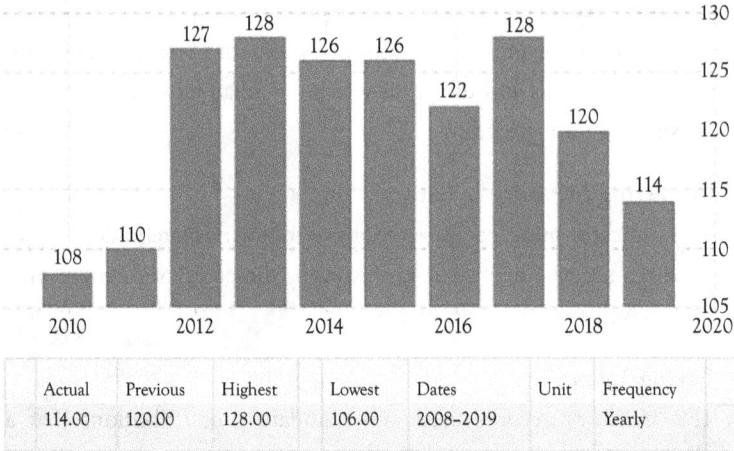

Actual	Previous	Highest	Lowest	Dates	Unit	Frequency
114.00	120.00	128.00	106.00	2008-2019		Yearly

Figure 11.3 The processes of changing electricity prices

Egypt Ranking When Compared With Other Countries in Research

New Zealand and Singapore once again landed in the top two spots of the global ranking, followed by Hong Kong, which rose one spot to edge out Denmark from third. Somalia retained its spot at the bottom of the chart, with its score actually falling slightly from last year's report. The UAE remains the highest ranked MENA country, despite falling to the 16th spot from 11 last years. Saudi Arabia was also the most-improved economy this year, soaring to the 62nd spot from 92 last year

Comparing Egypt Developing Areas 2020, 2019, and 2018

In 2020, Egypt concerned on four developing areas as mentioned earlier.

In 2019, Egypt concerned on five developing areas.

Getting credit—protecting minority investors—starting a business—paying taxes—resolving insolvency.

1n 2018, Egypt concerned on two developing areas.

Protecting minority investors—registering property.

Bibliography

Acs, Z. 1996. *Small Firms and Economic Growth*. Edward Elgar Publishing.

Acs, Z.J., and D.B. Audretsch. 1990. *Innovation and Small Firms*. Mit Press.

Acs, Z.J., and J.E. Amorós. 2008. "Entrepreneurship and Competitiveness Dynamics in Latin America." *Small Business Economics* 31, no. 3, pp. 305–322.

Acs, Z.J., and L. Preston. 1997. "Small and Medium-Sized Enterprises, Technology, and Globalization: Introduction to a Special Issue on Small and Medium-Sized Enterprises in the Global Economy." *Small Business Economics, 9*, no. 1, pp. 1–6.

Acs, Z.J., and L. Szerb. 2011. *Global Entrepreneurship and Development Index 2011*." Edward Elgar Publishing.

Adebanjo, D., R. Mann, M. Mohammad, and S.A. Bareduan. January 08, 2019. "A Study of the Activities and Impact of the Asian Productivity Organisation (APO)." *International Journal of Productivity and Performance Management* 68, no. 2, Article 1741–0401. www.emerald.com/insight/content/doi/10.1108/IJPPM-09-2017-0227/full/html

Aidis, R., S. Estrin, and T. Mickiewicz. 2008. "Institutions and Entrepreneurship Development in Russia: A Comparative Perspective." *Journal of Business Venturing* 23, no. 6, pp. 656–672.

Akorsu, P.K., and D. Agyapong. 2012. "Alternative Model for Financing SMEs in Ghana." *International Journal of Arts and Commerce* 1, no. 5, pp. 136–148.

Akuru, U.B., and O.I. Okoro. 2014. "Economic Implications of Constant Power Outages on SMEs in Nigeria." *Journal of Energy in Southern Africa* 25, no. 3, pp. 47–61.

Ale Ebrahim, N., S. Ahmed, and Z. Taha. 2010. "SMEs; Virtual Research and Development (R&D) Teams and New Product Development: A Literature Review. *International Journal of the Physical Sciences* 5, no. 7, pp. 916–930.

Allen, K., and P. Economy. 2008. *Complete MBA for Dummies*. Wiley Publishing, Inc.

Allen, R.B. 2008. "Capital, Illegal Slaves, Indentured Labourers and the Creation of a Sugar Plantation Economy in Mauritius, 1810–60." *The Journal of Imperial and Commonwealth History* 36, no. 2, pp. 151–170.

Almeida, P., and B. Kogut. 1997. "The Exploration of Technological Diversity and Geographic Localization in Innovation: Start-Up Firms in the Semiconductor Industry." *Small Business Economics* 9, no. 1, pp. 21–31.

Altman, E.I. 1968. "Financial Ratios, Discriminant Analysis and the Prediction of Corporate Bankruptcy." *The Journal of Finance* 23, no. 4, pp. 589–609. DOI: j.1540-6261.1968.tb00843.x

Ames, M.D. 1983. *Small Business Management*. West Publishing Co.

Amin, M., and A. Islam. 2015. "Are Large Informal Firms More Productive Than the Small Informal Firms? Evidence From Firm-Level Surveys in Africa." *World Development* 74, pp. 374–385.

Andersen, H., I. Cobbold, and G. Lawrie. 2001. "Balanced scorecard implementation in SMEs: Reflection on Literature and Practice." In *4th SME international Conference, Allborg university, Denmark*.

Anderson, E.W. 1996. "Customer Satisfaction and Price Tolerance." *Marketing Letters* 7, no. 3, pp. 19–30.

Anderson, E.W., C. Fornell, and D.R. Lehmann. July 1994. "Customer Satisfaction, Market Share, and Profitability: Findings From Sweden." *Journal of Marketing* 58, pp. 53–66.

Anderson, E.W., C. Fornell, and S.K. Mazvancheryl. October 2004. "Customer Satisfaction and Shareholder Value." *Journal of Marketing* 68, pp. 172–85.

Anwar, M. 2018. "Business Model Innovation and SMEs performance—Does Competitive Advantage Mediate?" *International Journal of Innovation Management* 22, no. 7, p. 1850057.

Arasti, Z. 2011. "An Empirical Study on the Causes of Business Failure in Iranian Context." *African Journal of Business Management* 5, no. 17, pp. 7488–7498.

Ardic, O.P., N. Mylenko, and V. Saltane. 2011. "Small and Medium Enterprises: A Cross-Country Analysis With a New Data Set." *World Bank Policy Research Working Paper*, WPS 5538. World Bank. © World Bank. https://openknowledge.worldbank.org/handle/10986/3309 License: CC BY 3.0 IGO

Arnaud, B. 2018. "The 10 Most Common Reasons Why Startups Fail." www.eu-startups.com/2018/09/the-10-most-common-reasons-why-startups-fail/

Asheim, B.T., and A. Isaksen. 2003. "SMEs and the Regional Dimension of Innovation." In T.B. Asheim, A. Isaksen, C. Nauwelaers, and F. Tödtling (eds.), *Regional innovation policy for small-medium enterprises*, pp. 21–46. https://doi.org/10.4337/9781781009659.00011

Audretsch, D. B., and M.P. Feldman. 1996. "R & D Spillovers and the Geography of Innovation and Production." *The American economic review* 86, no. 3, pp. 630–640.

Bank, H.F.C. 2004. *World Investment News-Pre-report Ghana*. World Investment News.

Barringer, B.R., and D.W. Greening. 1998. "Small Business Growth Through Geographic Expansion: A Comparative Case Study." *Journal of Business Venturing* 13, no. 6, pp. 467–492.

Basu, A., M. Yulek, and M.A. Yulek. 2004. "Microfinance in Africa: Experience and Lessons From Selected African Countries." www.imf.org/en/Publications/WP/Issues/2016/12/31/Microfinance-in-Africa-Experience-and-Lessons-From-Selected-African-Countries-17710

Beaver, W.H. 1966. "Financial Ratios as Predictors of Failure." *Journal of Accounting Research* 4, pp. 71–111.

Beck, T., A. Demirguc-Kunt, and R. Levine. 2005. "SMEs, Growth, And Poverty: Cross-Country Evidence." Journal of Economic Growth 10, no. 3, pp. 199–229.

Beck, T., and A. Demirguc-Kunt. 2006. "Small and Medium-Size Enterprises: Access to Finance as a Growth Constraint." *Journal of Banking & finance* 30, no. 11, pp. 2931–2943.

Belchamber, G. 1995. "Anti/Economics: Touting the Benefits, Ignoring the costs.-comment on australia. Industry commission." *The Growth and Revenue Implications of Hilmer and Related Reforms Australian Rationalist* 38, pp. 54–58.

Bergmann, H., and R. Sternberg. 2007. "The Changing Face of Entrepreneurship in Germany." *Small Business Economics* 28, no. 2–3, pp. 205–221.

Berle, G. 1989. *The Do It Yourself Business Book*. Wiley Co.

Bjerke, B., and C. Hultman. 2004. *Entrepreneurial Marketing: The Growth of Small Firms in the New Economic Era*. Edward Elgar Publishing.

Bond, J.S. 1996. *Science and Engineering Indicators*. National Science Board. (No. PB-96-185905/XAB; NSB-96-21).

Bosma, N., and V. Schutjens. 2010. "Understanding Regional Variation in Entrepreneurial Activity and Entrepreneurial Attitude in Europe." *Annals of Regional Science*, pp. 1–32.

Bouri, A., M. Breij, M. Diop, R. Kempner, B. Klinger, and K. Stevenson. November 2011. *Report on Support to SMEs in Developing Countries Through Financial Intermediaries*." Dalberg.

Brixy, U., R. Sternberg, and H. Stüber. 2012. "The Selectiveness of the Entrepreneurial Process." *Journal of Small Business Management* 50, no. 1, pp. 105–131.

Chandler, A.D. 1990. "The Enduring Logic of Industrial Success." *Harvard Business Review* 68, no. 2, pp. 130–140.

Chatterjee, D., V.J. Richardson, and R.W. Zmud. 2001. "Examining the Shareholder Wealth Effects of Announcements of Newly Created C. I. O. Positions." *MIS Quarterly* 25, no. 1, pp. 43–47.

Chiam, S.C., K.C. Tan, and A.A. Mamun. March 2009. "A Memetic Model of Evolutionary PSO for Computational Finance Applications." *Expert Systems with Applications* 36, no. 2, pp. 3695–3711.

Clement, J. 2020. *United States: Number of Internet Users 2000-2019*.

Cohen, W.M., and S. Klepper. 1996. "A Reprise of Size and R&D." *The Economic Journal* 106, no. 437, pp. 925–951.

Coviello, N.E., P.P. McDougall, and B.M. Oviatt. 2011. "The Emergence, Advance and Future of International Entrepreneurship Research: An Introduction to the Special Forum." *Journal of Business Venturing* 26, no. 6, pp. 625–631.

Curran, J., R. Rutherfoord, and S.L. Smith. 2000. "Is There a Local Business Community? Explaining the Non-Participation of Small Business in Local Economic Development." *Local Economy* 15, no. 2, pp. 128–143.

Danis, W.M., D. De Clercq, and O. Petricevic. 2011. "Are Social Networks More Important for New Business Activity in Emerging Than Developed Economies? An Empirical Extension." *International Business Review* 20, no. 4, pp. 394–408.

Davidson, R.J. 2004. "What Does the Prefrontal Cortex "Do" in Affect: Perspectives on Frontal EEG Asymmetry Research." *Biological Psychology* 67, no. 1–2, pp. 219–234.

De la Mothe, J., and G. Paquete, eds. 1996. *Evolutionary Economics and the New International Political Economy*, Vol. 1. Psychology Press.

DeSarbo, W.S., M. Wedel, M. Vriens, and V. Ramaswamy. 1992. Latent Class Metric Conjoint Analysis." *Marketing Letters* 3, no. 3, pp. 273–288.

Dhliwayo, S., and J.J. Van Vuuren. 2007. "The Strategic Entrepreneurial Thinking Imperative." *Acta Commercii* 7, no. 1. https://hdl.handle.net/10520/EJC17005

Dunnette, M.D., and L.M. Hough. 1990. *Handbook of Industrial and Organizational Psychology* (2nd ed.). Consulting Psychologist.

Dunning, D. 1995. "Trait Importance And Modifiability As Factors Influencing Self-Assessment And Self-Enhancement Motives." *Personality and Social Psychology Bulletin 21*, no. 12, pp. 1297–1306

Dunning, J.H. 1993. "Internationalizing Porter's Diamond." *MIR: Management International Review*, pp. 7–15.

Dweck, C.S. 2000. *Self-Theories: Their Role in Motivation, Personality, and Development*. Psychology Press.

Dweck, C.S. 2006. "Mindset: The new psychology of success." Random House Publishing.

Eden, L., E. Levitas, and R.J. Martinez. 1997. "The Production, Transfer and Spillover of Technology: Comparing Large and Small Multinationals as Technology Producers." *Small Business Economics* 9, no. 1, pp. 53–66.

El Seoud, A., M. Sayed, F.M. Kreishan, and M.A.M. Ali. 2019. "The Reality of SMEs in Arab Nations: Experience of Egypt, Jordan and Bahrain." *Journal of Islamic Financial Studies* 5, no. 2.

El Shobery, M.M., M.A. El-Iskandrani, and M.M.H. Hegazy. 2010. "Improving Organizational Performance of Small and Medium Enterprises in Egypt Through Promoting the Human Factors in Quality Management Systems." *International Journal of Business and Management*.

Eno-Obong, H. 2006. "Challenges of Entrepreneurship in Home Economics and Enhancement Strategies." *Journal of Home Economics Research* 7, pp. 69–75.

Faltin, G. 2007. *The Successful Entrepreneurs Start as an Artist and Composer*. German Industry and Commerce.

Franco, F., and H. Haase. December 2010. "Failure Factors in Small and Medium-Sized Enterprises, Qualitative Study From an Attributional Perspective." *International Entrepreneurship Management Journal* 6, pp. 503–523. DOI:10.1007/S11365-009-0124-5

Frydman, H., E.I. Altman, and D.L. Kao. 1985. "Introducing Recursive Partitioning for Financial Classification: The Case of Financial Distress." *Journal of Finance* 40, no. 1, pp. 269–291.

Gallup. 2014. *Starved of Financing, New Businesses Are in Decline.* Retrieved June 10, 2017 from https://news.gallup.com/businessjournal/175499/starved-financing-new-businesses-decline.aspx.

Gamage, A. S. 2003. "Small and Medium Enterprise Development in Sri Lanka: A Review." *Meijo Review* 3, no. 4, pp. 133–150.

Garfield, D.J., K.E. Moore, and R.L. Adams. 2019. *New Approaches to Energy Hardware Innovation and Incubation*(No. NREL/MP-6A65-73438). National Renewable Energy Lab.(NREL), Golden, CO (United States).

Gaskill L.R., H.E. Van Auken, and R.A. Manning. 1993. "A Factor Analytic Study of the Perceived Causes of Small Business Failure." *Journal of Small Business Management* 34, no. 4, pp. 18–31.

GEM, G.E.M. and A. Vanags. 2018. Global Entrepreneurship Monitor (GEM).

Gerber, M.E. 1995. *The E-Myth Revisited. Why Most Small Businesses Don't Work and What to Do About It.* HarperBusiness.

Gewehr, W.H. 1996. "The Information Dissemination Policy of the United States Patent and Trademark Office." *World Patent Information* 18, no. 2, pp. 61–67.

Gomes-Casseres, B. 1996. *The Alliance Revolution: The New Shape of Business Rivalry.* Harvard University Press.

Graham, P.G. 1999. "Small Business Participation in the Global Economy." *European Journal of Marketing*

Graham, P.G. 1999. "Small Business Participation in the Global Economy." *European journal of Marketing* 33, nos. (1/2), p. 88. ISSN: 0309-0566.

Harrison, A.E. 1994. "Productivity, Imperfect Competition and Trade Reform: Theory and Evidence." *Journal of International Economics* 36, no. 1–2, pp. 53–73.

Herath, H.A., and R. Mahmood. 2013. "Strategic Orientation Based Research Model of SME Performance for Developing Countries." *Review of Integrative Business and Economics Research* 2, no. 1, pp. 430–440.

Humphrey, J. 2003. *Opportunities for SMEs in Developing Countries to Upgrade in a Global Economy.* International Labour Organization.

Isenberg, D. 2011. "The Entrepreneurship Ecosystem Strategy as a New Paradigm for Economic Policy: Principles for Cultivating Entrepreneurship." *Presentation at the Institute of International and European Affairs* 1, no. 781, pp. 1–13.

Jaffe, A.B., M. Trajtenberg, and R. Henderson. 1993. "Geographic Localization of Knowledge Spillovers as Evidenced by Patent Citations." *The Quarterly Journal of Economics* 108, no. 3, pp. 577–598.

Johnson, D., and C. Turner. 2010. *International Business: Themes and Issues in the Modern Global Economy*. Routledge.

Johnson, V.D. 2009. *Growth Mindset as a Predictor of Smoking Cessation*. ETD Archive. 148. https://engagedscholarship.csuohio.edu/etdarchive/148

Jolene (2005). The Importance of Entrepreneurship. Measuring Entrepreneurship: A Digest of Indicators. [online]. http://www.oecd.org/dataoecd/53/24/41664503.pdf

Jutla, D., P. Bodorik, and J. Dhaliwal. 2002. "Supporting the E-Business Readiness of Small and Medium-Sized Enterprises: Approaches and Metrics." *Internet Research* 12, no. 2, pp. 139–164. DOI:10.1108/10662240210422512.

Kachembere, J. 2011. "SMEs Hold Key to Economic Growth." *The Standard*, p. 23.

Kamo, M. 2020. https://articles.bplans.com/6-reasons-your-small-business-will-fail-and-how-to-avoid-them/

Kersten, R., J. Harms, K. Liket, and K. Maas. 2017. "Small Firms, Large Impact? A Systematic Review of the SME Finance Literature." *World Development* 97, pp. 330–348.

Keskǧn, H., C. Ǧentirk, O. Sungur, and H.M. Kǧrǧǧ. June 08–09, 2010. "The Importance of SMEs in Developing Economies." In *Proceedings of the 2nd International Symposium on Sustainable Development*, Sarajevo, Bosnia and Herzegovina, pp. 183–192.

Ketkar, S., and Z.J. Acs. 2013. "Where Angels Fear to Tread: Internationalization of Emerging Country SMEs." *Journal of International Entrepreneurship* 11, no. 3, pp. 201–219.

Kim, H.S. 2005. "Consumer Profiles of Apparel Product Involvement and Values." *Journal of Fashion Marketing and Management* 9, no. 2, pp. 207–220.

Kiyosaki, R., and S. Lechter. 2003. *The Cashflow Quadrant*. Grand Central Publishing.

Klapper, L., L. Laeven, and R. Rajan. 2006. "Entry Regulation as a Barrier to Entrepreneurship." *Journal of Financial Economics* 82, no. 3, pp. 591–629.

Kohn, S., and S. Hüsig. 2006. "Potential Benefits, Current Supply, Utilization And Barriers to Adoption: An Exploratory Study on German SMEs and Innovation Software." *Technovation* 26, no. 8, pp. 988–998.

Kolari, J., D. Glennon, H. Shin, and M. Caputo. 2002. "Predicting Large Us Commercial Bank Failures." *Journal of Economic Business* 54, pp. 361–387.

La Porta, R., and A. Shleifer. 2008. *The Unofficial Economy and Economic Development*. National Bureau of Economic Research.

Laforet, S. 2008. "Size, Strategic, and Market Orientation Affects on Innovation." *Journal of Business Research* 61, no. 7, pp. 753–764.

Linkov, I., T. Bridges, F. Creutzig, J. Decker, C. Fox-Lent, W. Krgöger, and T. Thiel-Clemen. 2014. "Changing the Resilience Paradigm." *Nature Climate Change* 4, no. 6, pp. 407–409.

Lotito, V., L Spinosa, G. Mininni, and R. Antonacci. 1997. The Theology of Sewage Sludge at Different Steps of Treatment." *Water Science and Technology* 36, no. 11, pp. 79–85.

Lu, J.W., and P.W. Beamish. 2001. "The Internationalization and Performance of SMEs." *Strategic Management Journal* 22, no. 6–7, pp. 565–586.

Lukács, E. 2005. "The Economic Role of SMEs in World Economy, Especially in Europe." *European Integration Studies* 4, no. 1, pp. 3–12.

Madrid-Guijarro, A., D. García-Pérez-de-Lema, and H. Van Auken. 2013. "An Investigation of Spanish SME Innovation During Different Economic Conditions." *Journal of Small Business Management* 51, no. 4, pp. 578–601.

Makino, S., and A. Delios. 1996. Local Knowledge Transfer and Performance: Implications for Alliance Formation in Asia." *Journal of International Business Studies* 27, no. 5, pp. 905–927.

Mambula, C. 2002. "Perceptions of SME Growth Constraints in Nigeria." *Journal of Small Business Management* 40, no. 1, pp. 58–65.

Martin, D. 1977. "Early Warning of Bank Failure." *Journal of Banking Finance* 1, pp. 249–276.

McGrath, R., and I. MacMillian. 2000. *The Entrepreneurial Mindset: Strategies for Continuously Creating Opportunity in an Age of Uncertainty.* Harvard Business Press.

Metzger, G. 2014. *Gründungstätigkeit wiederbelebt—Impuls aus dem Nebenerwerb.*

Mike Kamo. 2020. https://articles.bplans.com/6-reasons-your-small-business-will-fail-and-how-to-avoid-them/

Molden, D.C., and C.S. Dweck. 2006. "Finding 'Meaning' in Psychology: A Lay Theories Approach to Self-Regulation, Social Perception, and Social Development." *American Psychologist* 61, no. 3, p. 192.

Morris, M.H., and D.F. Kuratko. 2002. *Corporate Entrepreneurship: Entrepreneurial Development Within Organizations.* South-Western Pub.

Muritala, T., A. Awolaja, and Y. Bako. 2012. "Impact of Small and Medium Enterprises on Economic Growth and Development." *American Journal of Business and Management* 1, no. 1, pp. 18–22.

National Science Foundation (US). Directorate for Education & Human Resources. 1996. *Shaping the Future: New Expectations for Undergraduate Education in Science, Mathematics, Engineering, and Technology* (Vol. 1). National Science Foundation, Division of Undergraduate Education.

Ndiaye, N., L.A. Razak, R. Nagayev, and A. Ng. 2018. "Demystifying Small and Medium Enterprises (SMEs) Performance in Emerging and Developing Economies." *Borsa Istanbul Review* 18, no. 4, pp. 269–281.

Neneh, B.N. 2011. "The Impact of Entrepreneurial Characteristics and Business Practices on the Long-Term Survival of SMEs."

Nieman, G. 2006. "Managing the Small Business. A South African Approach." Van Schaik Publishers.

Nissan, E., M. Castaño, and I. Carrasco. 2012. "Drivers of Non-Profit Activity: A Cross-Country Analysis." *Small Business Economics* 38, no. 3, pp. 303–320.

North, D. 1990. *Institutions, Institutional Change, and Economic Performance.* Cambrige University Press.

O'Connor, E.J., and C.M. Fiol. 2002. "Mindful Over Mindless: Learning to Think Like an Entrepreneur." *Physician Executive* 28, no. 4, pp. 18–23.

Okoro, C.B., E.B. Ewah, and S.C. Ndema. 2020. "Failure and Success of Entrepreneurs in Nigeria: An Empirical Review." *International Academic Journal of Business School Research* 8, no. 4, pp. 1–21.

Olawale, F., and D. Garwe. 2010. "Obstacles to the Growth of New SMEs in South Africa: A Principal Component Analysis Approach." *African Journal of Business Management* 4, no. 5, pp. 729–738.

Organisation for Economic Co-operation and Development Staff. 2005. *OECD Factbook 2005: Economic, Environmental and Social Statistics.* OECD.

Ozkan, I., I. Türkşen, and N.A. Canpolat. 2008. "Currency Crisis and Its Perception With Fuzzy C-Means." *Information Sciences* 178, pp. 1923–1934.

Paffenholz, G. 1998. "Krisenhafte entwicklungen in mittelständischen unternehmen." *Ursachenanalyse und Implikationen für die Beratung.* IfM-Materialien Nr. 130.

Pandya, V.M. September 2012. "Comparative Analysis of Development of SMEs in Developed and Developing Countries." *The 2012 International Conference on Business and Management,* pp. 6–7.

Pokharel, S., K.T Yeo, and T.Y. Wang. 2006. "Value of Project Management in High-Tech and Manufacturing Operations." *Journal of the Chinese Institute of Industrial Engineers* 23, no. 6, pp. 443–448.

Pomare, C. 2018. "A Multiple Framework Approach to Sustainable Development Goals (SDGs) and Entrepreneurship: Entrepreneurship and the Sustainable Development Goals." *Contemporary Issues in Entrepreneurship Research* 8, pp. 11–31.

Rafinejad, D. 2007. *Innovation Development and Commercialization of New Products: Case Studies and Key Practices for Market Leadership.* J ROSS publishing.

Rand, J., and N. Torm. 2012. "The Benefits of Formalization: Evidence From Vietnamese Manufacturing SMEs." *World Development* 40, no. 5, pp. 983–998.

Raymond, L., and J. St-Pierre. 2004. "Customer Dependency in Manufacturing SMEs: Implications for R&D and Performance." *Journal of Small Business and Enterprise Development* 11, no. 1, pp. 23–33. DOI: 10.1108/14626000410519074

Reynolds, P., N. Bosma, E. Autio, S. Hunt, N. De Bono, I. Servais, P. Lopez-Garcia, and N. Chin. 2005. "Global Entrepreneurship Monitor: Data Collection Design and Implementation 1998–2003." *Small Business Economics* 24, no. 3, pp. 205–231.

Ricupero, R., A. Warner, S. Narain, C. Güttler, L. Kasekende, M. Zouari, R. Kloeppinger-Todd, R. Narasimham, J. Bays, and B. Dunsby. 2001. "Improving the Competitiveness of SMEs in Developing Countries. The Role of Finance to Enhance Enterprise Development." In United Nations Conference on Trade and Development, pp. 59–143.

Scarborough, N.M. 2016. *Essentials of Entrepreneurship and Small Business Management*. Pearson.

Schaefer, J.L., J.C.M. Siluk, P.S.D. Carvalho, J. Renes Pinheiro, and P.S. Schneider. 2020. "Management Challenges and Opportunities for Energy Cloud Development and Diffusion." *Energies* 13, no. 16, p. 40–48.

Scheepers, D. 2009. "Turning Social Identity Threat Into Challenge: Status Stability and Cardiovascular Reactivity During Inter-Group Competition." *Journal of Experimental Social Psychology* 45, no. 1, pp. 228–233.

Second OECD Conference of Ministers responsible for Small and Medium-sized Enterprises (SMEs). June 03–05, 2004. "Promoting Entrepreneurship and Innovative SMEs in a Global Economy: Towards a More Responsible and Inclusive Globalisation." Istanbul, Turkey.

Simpson, M., and N. Taylor. 2002. "The Role and Relevance of Marketing in SMEs: Towards a New Model." *Journal of small Business and Enterprise Development* 9, no. 4, pp. 370–382. DOI:10.1108/14626000210450559

Singh, R.K., S.K. Garg, and S.G. Deshmukh. 2010. "The Competitiveness of SMEs in a Globalized Economy." *Management Research Review* 33, no. 1, p. 54.

Sinitsyn, N.A., J.E. Hill, H. Min, J. Sinova, and A.H. MacDonald. 2018. "Charge and Spin Hall Conductivity in Metallic Graphene." *Physical Review Letters* 97, no. 10, p. 106804.

Sodagar, B. (2006). [Design of] Woodland Sustainable Community Hall, Hill Holt Wood, Lincolnshire.

Small Business Service. 2001. *SME Statistics for the UK, 2000*. SBS.

Smith, D.R., W.J. Padilla, D.C. Vier, S.C. Nemat-Nasser, and S. Schultz. 2000. "Composite Medium With Simultaneously Negative Permeability and Permittivity." *Physical Review Letters* 84, no. 18, p. 4184.

Staniewski, M., and K. Awruk. 2015. "Motivating Factors and Barriers in the Commencement of One's Own Business for Potential Entrepreneurs." *Economic Research-Ekonomska Istraživanja* 28, no. 1, pp. 583–592.

Stinchcombe, A. 1965. "Organization-Creating Organizations." *Society* 2, no. 2, pp. 34–35.

Taiwo, J.N., T.O. Falohun, and P.E. Agwu. 2016. "SMEs Financing and Its Effects on Nigerian Economic Growth." *European Journal of Business, Economics and Accountancy* 4, no. 4.

Tam, K.Y. 1991. "Neural Network Models and the Prediction of Bank Bankruptcy." *Omega* 19, pp. 429–445.

Thabit, T.H., and M.B. Raewf. 2015. "The Impact of Voluntary Disclosure on SMEs in Developing Countries." *6th International Conference on Global Social Entrepreneurship* (Kota Bharu).

The Economist. 2009. www.economist.com/theworldin/2009.

Thompson Agyapong, G., F. Mmieh, and C. Mordi. 2018. "Factors Influencing the Growth of SMEs: The Case of Ghana." *Thunderbird International Business Review* 60, no. 4, pp. 549–563.

Timmons J.A., and S. Spinelli. 2004. *New Venture Creation: Entrepreneurship for the 21st century*. McGraw Hill Irwin.

Timmons, J.A. 1994. *New Venture Creation: Entrepreneurship for the 21st century*. Irwin.

Troilo, M. 2011. "Legal Institutions and High-Growth Aspiration Entrepreneurship." *Economic Systems* 35, no. 2, pp. 158–175.

Van Roy, V., and D. Nepelski. 2017. "Determinants of High-Tech Entrepreneurship in Europe." Joint Research Centre, JRC Scientific and Policy Reports—EUR 28299 EN.

Waita, S.M., and G.S. Namusonge. 2013. "Entrepreneurial Motivation as a Factor Affecting Small and Medium Enterprises Performance in the Coffee Subsector in Kenya. Study of Tropical Farm Management Kenya limited." *International Journal of Academic Research, Business and Social Sciences* 3, no. 12.

Walsh, G.S., and J. Cunningham. 2016. "Business Failure and Entrepreneurship." *Emergence, Evolution and Future Research* 12, no. 3, pp. 163–285.

Wang, Y. 2016. "What Are the Biggest Obstacles to Growth of SMEs in Developing Countries? An Empirical Evidence From an Enterprise Survey." *Borsa Istanbul Review* 16, no. 3, pp. 167–176.

Woywode, M. 1998. *Determinanten der Überlebenswahrscheinlichkeit von Unternehmen*, ZEW Wirtschaftsanalysen, Bd. 25. Baden-Baden.

Xhepa, S. 2006. *Competitiveness and the SME Development in Albania*. The Institute for Contemporary Studies (ISB).

Yeung, Z.J.Á.B. 1999. *Small and Medium-Sized Enterprises in the Global Economy*. University of Michigan Press.

Yunpeng Zhu, H.H. 2006. *The East Asian High-Tech Drive*. Edward Elgar Publishing.

Zhang, D., M. Hu, and Q. Ji. 2020. "Financial Markets Under the Global Pandemic of COVID-19." *Finance Research Letters* 36, p. 101528.

Zmijewski, M.E. 1984. "Methodological Issues Related to the Estimation of Financial Distress Prediction Models." *Journal of Accounting Research* 22, pp. 59–82.

About the Author

Amr Sukkar, PhD, MBA, Management Consultant, is a management associate professor at LIGS University (Hawaii, United States) and business economist expert at the European Union. He also manages/directs a leading medical company and teaches management for MBA and DBA programs at different business schools as well as public administration and management at several prestigious international and local universities. Sukkar develops and delivers training programs (entrepreneurship, SMEs, and strategic management). In addition, he is a subject matter expert at the National Training Academy (NTA) at the Egyptian presidential office. Moreover, he is a project and strategic management consultant for several organizations. He is experienced in international and multinational corporates. He developed a new model for sustainability leadership for Middle East SMEs in his PhD thesis and published articles focused on SMEs, leadership, governances, and sustainable development in international scientific journals. The Author of "Sustainability Leader in Green Business Era" Book author.

Author Contact Information

Amr Sukkar PhD, M Phil, MBA

Management Consultant Strategic Management Associate Professor

E-Mail: amressamsukkar@gmail.com, amr.sukkar@ligsuniversity.com
LinkedIn: https://www.linkedin.com/in/amr-sukkar-a6301818

YouTube: https://youtube.com/channel/UCBggPEhdf62bsNq5H ChaSgg

Research: https://www.researchgate.net/profile/Amr-Sukkar/research

https://scholar.google.com/scholar?hl=en&as_sdt=0%2C5&q=Amr +Sukkar&btnG=

Index

OTHER TITLES IN THE ECONOMICS AND PUBLIC POLICY COLLECTION

Jeffrey Edwards, North Carolina A&T State University, Editor

- *Rebooting Local Economies* by Robert Pittman, Rhonda Phillips, and Amanda Sutt
- *The Language of Value* by Virginia B. Robertson
- *Transparency in ESG and the Circular Economy* by Dolan Cristina and Barrero Zalles Diana
- *Developing Sustainable Energy Projects in Emerging Markets* by Francis Ugboma
- *Understanding the Indian Economy from the Post-Reforms of 1991, Volume III* by Shrawan Kumar Singh
- *Understanding Economic Equilibrium* by Mike Shaw, Thomas J. Cunningham, and Rosemary Cunningham
- *Business Liability and Economic Damages, Second Edition* by Scott D. Gilbert
- *Macroeconomics, Third Edition* by David G. Tuerck
- *Negotiation Booster* by Kasia Jagodzinska
- *Mastering the Moneyed Mind, Volume IV* by Christopher Bayer
- *Mastering the Moneyed Mind, Volume III* by Christopher Bayer
- *Mastering the Moneyed Mind, Volume II* by Christopher Bayer
- *Mastering the Moneyed Mind, Volume I* by Christopher Bayer
- *Understanding the Indian Economy from the Post-Reforms of 1991, Volume II* by Shrawan Kumar Singh

Concise and Applied Business Books

The Collection listed above is one of 30 business subject collections that Business Expert Press has grown to make BEP a premiere publisher of print and digital books. Our concise and applied books are for...

- Professionals and Practitioners
- Faculty who adopt our books for courses
- Librarians who know that BEP's Digital Libraries are a unique way to offer students ebooks to download, not restricted with any digital rights management
- Executive Training Course Leaders
- Business Seminar Organizers

Business Expert Press books are for anyone who needs to dig deeper on business ideas, goals, and solutions to everyday problems. Whether one print book, one ebook, or buying a digital library of 110 ebooks, we remain the affordable and smart way to be business smart. For more information, please visit www.businessexpertpress.com, or contact sales@businessexpertpress.com.

www.ingramcontent.com/pod-product-compliance
Lightning Source LLC
Chambersburg PA
CBHW061321220326
41599CB00026B/4977